THE SWEET MELISSA BAKING BOOK

THE SWEET MELISSA BAKING BOOK

Recipes from the Beloved Bakery
for Everyone's Favorite Treats

MELISSA MURPHY

VIKING STUDIO

VIKING STUDIO
Published by the Penguin Group
Penguin Group (USA) Inc., 375 Hudson Street,
New York, New York 10014, U.S.A.
Penguin Group (Canada), 90 Eglinton Avenue East, Suite 700,
Toronto, Ontario, Canada M4P 2Y3
(a division of Pearson Penguin Canada Inc.)
Penguin Books Ltd, 80 Strand, London WC2R 0RL, England
Penguin Ireland, 25 St. Stephen's Green, Dublin 2, Ireland
(a division of Penguin Books Ltd)
Penguin Books Australia Ltd, 250 Camberwell Road,
Camberwell, Victoria 3124, Australia
(a division of Pearson Australia Group Pty Ltd)
Penguin Books India Pvt Ltd, 11 Community Centre,
Panchsheel Park, New Delhi – 110 017, India
Penguin Group (NZ), 67 Apollo Drive, Rosedale, North Shore 0632,
New Zealand (a division of Pearson New Zealand Ltd)
Penguin Books (South Africa) (Pty) Ltd, 24 Sturdee Avenue,
Rosebank, Johannesburg 2196, South Africa

Penguin Books Ltd, Registered Offices:
80 Strand, London WC2R 0RL, England

First published in 2008 by Viking Studio,
a member of Penguin Group (USA) Inc.

1 3 5 7 9 10 8 6 4 2

Color photographs by Miha Matei
Black and white photographs by Johannes Kroemer
Food styling by Anna Elisa de Castro

LIBRARY OF CONGRESS CATALOGING IN PUBLICATION DATA
Murphy, Melissa.
The Sweet Melissa baking book : recipes from the beloved bakery for everyone's favorite treats / Melissa Murphy.
p. cm.
Includes index.
ISBN 978-0-670-01874-1
1. Desserts. 2. Baking. 3. Sweet Melissa Pâtisserie. I. Title.
TX773.M9 2008
641.8'6—dc22   2007032338

Printed in the United States of America
Set in Helvetica LT Standard
Designed by Katy Riegel

To my mom, who has been with me to hold my hand every step of the way

To both of my dads, whose belief in me has made me feel that no dream is too big

To all of my brothers and sisters, without whom my fondest memories wouldn't exist

To my staff, whose loyalty and dedication are unsurpassed

And to Chris, whose encouragement and unconditional love remain constant

CONTENTS

INTRODUCTION

ONE OF MY favorite Murphy family outings was our annual fall pilgrimage to the apple orchards in upstate New York. There, my brothers, and later my sister too, and I would climb the trees in search of the biggest and reddest apples we could find. After each trip, we'd come home and spend hours jarring our own cinnamon applesauce, days experimenting with other apple recipes, and weeks scratching our poison ivy.

My mom and I would always make the pies. She taught me to roll pie dough before I could recite the alphabet. Whenever we made a pie, I'd make a small one all for myself—I'd sweeten the apples the way I liked them, putting much too much cinnamon in the filling, and I'd roll out the top crust and crimp the edge with my knuckle into my fingertips. Once it went into the oven, I'd open the door a hundred

times to see if my little pie was bubbling. I remember how proud I was when it was ready and I could taste all those tender cinnamon apples. My mom would assure me that my pie was much, much better than hers.

I fell in love with baking through experiences such as this as a child, but it took working in a restaurant for me to realize that this was something I wanted to do professionally. Throughout my years in college, I worked at a place on the Upper West Side called Panarella's. I started working as a server and was soon asked to hostess and assist the manager, and then to be the manager. After many nights watching Raoul, the pastry chef, simultaneously brûlée custards while plating lemon tarts with raspberry sauce, I asked him one day if I could give it a try. I knew right away that I belonged in the kitchen. So I enrolled at the French Culinary Institute.

After I graduated, I was lucky to live in New York City and found myself working under some talented chefs. My first professional cooking job was with a catering company named Foodstyle, which served a very distinguished clientele, mainly fashion photographers and models working for *Glamour* and *Vogue.* Foodstyle's food struck me as very home cooked: fresh and delicious but not exactly trendy. I didn't really get it until the owner sent me on a lunch delivery to one of the studios. When I gave the client his meal and told him we'd made black bottom brownies for dessert, he literally jumped up and down, clapping his hands. It was then that I understood. The best food doesn't have to be challenging in its preparation, but should recall our fondest food memories.

After Foodstyle, I went to work for David Page and Barbara Shinn at Home Restaurant in the West Village. Was this place *tiny*! Was this food *delicious*! David took "homemade" to the next level, making his own salami and duck sausage; he even made his own ketchup! I remember one evening, must've been a Monday (the restaurant's only day of rest), David and Barbara had the kitchen to themselves and were "putting up" bourbon cherries. Those filled mason jars cooling on fresh towels made my heart ache for the days of canning fruit with my mom. That weekend I got some peaches, called Mom up, and we started canning just where we left off.

After leaving Home I worked in some lovely French restaurants, where I learned to make and respect what goes into a beautiful plated dessert. I applied many of the skills I learned at the FCI, like folding fluffy meringues into ground nuts to create crisp daquoise. I developed some wonderful menus based on French classics that were great successes, but at the end of the day, it was peach cobbler that I longed for.

The result of my formal training mixed with my love of homespun desserts is a style that is a French-influenced American approach to baking—where looks are important but it is the taste that wins the blue ribbon.

I opened my Sweet Melissa Pâtisserie ten years ago with this idea in mind. My opening menu included Lemon Tarts and Chestnut Honey Madeleines, Sweet Fruit Muffins and Sticky Buns with Toasted Almonds, Gingersnaps and Chocolate Chip Cookies, among a few others—it was small but special. Since these recipes are familiar to everyone, I needed them to be the best of their kind. As a result, everything that is baked at Sweet Melissa's is my favorite thing. The fun part is getting there, and a *lot* of testing goes into perfecting these recipes. Once I think I've gotten it, I try the recipe on my customers. I know when I've gotten it right: I see the person's eyes close as they bite into a gooey sticky bun or decadent piece of cake. They nod their head as they chew, and reluctantly swallow. Often there's an accompanying *hmmmming* sound. Then they smile when they open their eyes to see that there's enough left for another bite.

I create desserts that make people feel welcome when they walk into my shop. I love to hear them squeal with delight as they look at a beautifully decorated lemon cupcake or bite into the most deliciously perfect chocolate chip cookie. I'm not interested in desserts that involve ten components, exotic ingredients, and structural supports. I want to make everyone's favorite desserts better than they've had them before.

Now you can too.

THE SWEET MELISSA BAKING BOOK

CHAPTER ONE

DESSERT FOR BREAKFAST

Muffins, Quick Breads, and More

Sweet Muffins

Savory Muffins

Orange-Scented Scones

Guinness Gingerbread

Mom's Banana Apple Bread

Whole Orange–Poppy Seed Cake

Golden Almond Fruitcake

Sweet Potato Bread with Cinnamon-Rum-Orange Glaze

Mom's French Pancakes

Caramel Apple Turnovers with Sweet Ricotta Filling

Lemon Walnut–Sour Cream Pound Cake

Sweet Plum Clafoutis with Almonds

Hot Pepper Gingerbread Muffins with Orange Maple Butter

Cherry Almond Granola

Granola Breakfast Cookies

Irish Soda Bread

Sticky Buns with Toasted Almonds

Raised Waffles with Warm Brown Sugar Bananas

Bee Stings

I Love to Eat Chocolate Chip Cookies for Breakfast . . .

I LOVE TO EAT chocolate chip cookies for breakfast. I can't think of a better way to start the day than with a tall glass of cold milk and two homemade chocolate chip cookies—on the chewy side. I do occasionally stray from my first love, sometimes indulging in a hand-rolled croissant with strawberry jam, or a warm sticky bun oozing with cinnamon and dripping with sticky sauce. I am a pastry chef, after all. I try not to show favoritism in my choice of freshly baked treats.

In writing this book, I've realized that it may seem odd to some of you to eat dessert for breakfast, so I thought I'd disguise it. But really, who are we kidding? You love sticky buns first thing in the morning just as much as I do—I should know, after all, as each day I make them to sell in my shop and each day you buy them. But

you should give chocolate chip cookies a chance. Try one or two in the morning, and I bet you'll love them too. (Since most people don't eat their chocolate chip cookies in the morning as I do, I've put the recipe for some of the best you'll ever have in the After-School Snack chapter.)

SWEET MUFFINS

This is my standard sweet fruit muffin recipe. It works with a variety of fruits, spices, citrus zests, and herbs. Some of my favorite variations follow (see pages 6–7). Once you are comfortable with the basic recipe, you can play with any number of sweet things to create many delicious alternatives, from bananas and chocolate chips, to dried fruits and nuts.
Makes 12 muffins

2¾ cups all-purpose flour
1 tablespoon plus 1 teaspoon baking powder
½ cup granulated sugar
½ teaspoon kosher salt
8 tablespoons (1 stick) unsalted butter, melted
⅓ cup firmly packed light brown sugar
2 large eggs, at room temperature
¼ cup heavy cream, at room temperature
½ cup whole milk, at room temperature (see Note)
Zest of 1 lemon
1 cup fresh fruit, cut into ¼- to ½-inch pieces
1 tablespoon vanilla sugar (see Pro Tip) or granulated sugar, for sprinkling

BEFORE YOU START

Position a rack in the center of your oven. Preheat the oven to 350°F. Line a standard 12-cup muffin tin with muffin papers (or butter and flour the cups or spray with nonstick vegetable cooking spray).

1. In a large bowl, whisk together the flour, baking powder, granulated sugar, and salt. Set aside.

2. In a medium bowl, whisk together the melted butter, brown sugar, and eggs until smooth—no lumps. Whisk in the heavy cream and milk until combined.

3. Add the zest to the flour mixture and with your hands, gently rub the mixture together, releasing the oils and breaking up the bits. Add the fresh fruit and gently toss with your fingers to combine. Make a well in the center of the bowl. Pour the

butter mixture into the center of the well and, using a rubber spatula, gently pull the flour mixture into the center of the well until just combined.

4. Divide the batter evenly among the prepared muffin cups, filling each cup until full. Bake for 30 to 35 minutes, or until lightly golden and a wooden skewer inserted into the center comes out clean. Remove to a wire rack and sprinkle with sugar. Let cool to warm.

The muffins are best eaten the day they are made, but they can be tightly wrapped in plastic wrap and kept at room temperature for 2 days. For longer storage, wrap in plastic wrap and refrigerate for up to 5 days, or freeze well wrapped in plastic wrap and then aluminum foil for up to 3 weeks. Defrost still wrapped at room temperature.

Note: You will use more or less milk depending on the juiciness of the fruit.

Fresh Peach Muffins

Add ½ teaspoon ground cinnamon to the flour mixture. Decrease the milk by 2 tablespoons. Use 1½ teaspoons freshly grated orange zest to rub into the flour mixture. Add 1 cup peeled diced fresh peaches to the dry mixture, and proceed with the batter. Fill the prepared muffin cups and sprinkle on cinnamon sugar (see page 56), if desired. Bake as directed.

Strawberry Muffins with Fresh Lemon and Rosemary

Decrease the milk by 2 tablespoons. Use 1½ teaspoons freshly grated lemon zest and ¾ teaspoon finely chopped fresh rosemary to rub into the flour mixture. Add 1 cup diced fresh strawberries to the dry mixture, and proceed with the batter. Fill the prepared muffin cups and sprinkle on vanilla sugar (see Pro Tip), if desired. Bake as directed.

Orange Blueberry Muffins with Pecan Crumble

Add ¼ teaspoon ground nutmeg to the dry ingredients. Use 1½ teaspoons freshly grated orange zest to rub into the flour mixture. Add 1 cup fresh blueberries to the flour mixture, and proceed with the batter. Fill the prepared muffin cups and sprinkle on one-half recipe of Pecan Crumble (see page 160). Bake as directed.

Pear Cranberry Muffins with Gingersnap Crumble

Add ½ teaspoon freshly ground nutmeg to the flour ingredients. Use 1½ teaspoons freshly grated orange zest to rub into the flour mixture. Add ½ cup fresh or frozen cranberries and ¾ cup ripe peeled and diced Bosc pears to the flour mixture, and proceed with the batter. Fill the prepared muffin cups and sprinkle over one-half recipe Gingersnap Crumble (see page 148). Bake as directed.

PRO TIP: To make vanilla sugar, combine the split and scraped pod and seeds of 1 vanilla bean with 8 cups of sugar. Rub them together with your hands. Store in an airtight container.

SAVORY MUFFINS

OK, not everything we make at Sweet Melissa's is sweet. We also have a lovely savory menu with homemade soups, sandwiches, quiches, and frittatas. I want to share this recipe for savory muffins with you because they are just so popular every morning at the shop. Like the Sweet Muffins, this Savory Muffins recipe is the base for a wealth of yummy creations. Check out some of my favorites, which follow. Once you get to know this recipe, feel free to make up your own! We use sautéed spinach, roasted cauliflower and zucchini, different cheeses—you get the idea. These muffins are delicious all by themselves or served alongside soups and salads. **Makes 12 muffins**

3 cups all-purpose flour
1 tablespoon plus 1½ teaspoons baking powder
1½ teaspoons kosher salt
¾ teaspoon freshly ground black pepper
¼ teaspoon cayenne pepper
1 teaspoon sugar
10 tablespoons unsalted butter, melted
2 large eggs
½ cup heavy cream, at room temperature
½ cup whole milk, at room temperature
1 cup crumbled or shredded cheese
1 cup chopped cooked vegetables (¼- to ½-inch pieces) (or fruit, vegetables, sun-dried tomatoes, see variations that follow)

BEFORE YOU START

Position a rack in the center of your oven. Preheat the oven to 350°F. Line a standard 12-cup muffin tin with muffin papers (or butter and flour the cups or spray them with nonstick vegetable cooking spray).

1. In a large bowl, whisk together the flour, baking powder, salt, black pepper, cayenne, and sugar.

2. In a small bowl, whisk together the melted butter and eggs. Whisk in the heavy cream and milk until combined.

3. Add the cheese and chopped vegetables to the flour mixture and gently toss with your fingers to coat. Make a well in the center. Pour the butter mixture into the center of the well and, using a rubber spatula, gently pull the flour mixture into the center of the well until just combined.

4. Divide the batter evenly among the prepared muffin cups, filling each cup until full. Bake for 30 to 35 minutes, or until lightly golden and a wooden skewer inserted into the center comes out clean. Remove to a wire rack to cool.

Serve warm or at room temperature. The muffins are best eaten the day they are made, but they can be tightly wrapped in plastic wrap and kept for 2 days at room temperature. For longer storage, wrap in plastic wrap and refrigerate for up to 5 days, or freeze well wrapped in plastic wrap and then aluminum foil for up to 3 weeks. Defrost still wrapped at room temperature.

Goat Cheese, Olive, and Thyme Muffins

Combine 1 cup crumbled fresh goat cheese, ¾ cup pitted coarsely chopped Kalamata olives, and 1 tablespoon chopped fresh thyme over the combined flour mixture and toss gently. Proceed as directed.

Caramelized Onion, Sage, and Cheddar Muffins

Sprinkle 1 cup chopped caramelized onions, 2 tablespoons chopped fresh sage, and 1 cup shredded sharp cheddar cheese over the combined flour mixture and toss gently. Proceed as directed.

Bosc Pear, Blue Cheese, and Walnut Muffins

Sprinkle 1 cup peeled, cored, and chopped Bosc pears (instead of the vegetables); ¾ cup crumbled blue cheese and ½ cup coarsely chopped, lightly toasted walnuts over the combined flour mixture and toss gently. Proceed as directed.

Sun-Dried Tomatoes, Feta, and Oregano Muffins

Sprinkle 1 cup drained chopped sun-dried tomatoes (packed in olive oil); 1 cup crumbled feta cheese; and 1½ tablespoons chopped fresh oregano over the combined flour mixture and toss gently. Proceed as directed.

ORANGE-SCENTED SCONES

For the longest time I wouldn't give up this recipe, which is significant because I was taught early on to share recipes. I love what the homemade oat flour does to the texture—the scones are flakey in an I-can't-quite-put-my-finger-on-it way. At Sweet Melissa's, they are the star of afternoon tea, delicious when served with double cream and homemade jumbleberry preserves. **Makes 6 scones**

FOR THE SCONES
8 tablespoons (1 stick) cold unsalted butter
½ cup oat flour or ⅔ cup whole oats (to be ground)
1½ cups all-purpose flour
2 teaspoons baking powder
½ teaspoon kosher salt
1 tablespoon sugar
2 teaspoons freshly grated orange zest
⅔ cup heavy cream
1 large egg

FOR THE GLAZE
2 tablespoons heavy cream
1 tablespoon sugar

BEFORE YOU START

Place a rack in the center of your oven. Preheat the oven to 350°F. Line a cookie sheet with parchment paper or aluminum foil.

TO MAKE THE SCONES

1. Cut the cold butter into ½-inch pieces. Keep refrigerated.

2. If using the oat flour, place the flour in the bowl of a food processor. If using the whole oats, place the oats in the bowl of a food processor and pulse to a coarse flour. Add the all-purpose flour, baking powder, salt, sugar, and zest, and pulse to combine. Add the chilled butter pieces and pulse until the size of medium peas. (At

this point, the mixture can be stored in an airtight container in the refrigerator for up to 1 week or in the freezer for up to 1 month.)

3. In a medium bowl, whisk together the heavy cream and egg until smooth. Fold the flour mixture into the egg mixture to combine; the dough should hold together. Don't overmix.

4. Turn the dough out onto a lightly floured work surface and pat into a flattened round disk measuring 7 inches across. Using a sharp knife, cut the disk (pie style) into 6 even triangles. Place at least 2 inches apart on the prepared cookie sheet.

5. *For the glaze:* Brush the scones with the heavy cream and sprinkle with the sugar.

6. Bake for 30 minutes, or until lightly golden. Remove to a wire rack to cool.

The scones are best eaten the day they are made, but can be frozen tightly wrapped in plastic wrap and then aluminum foil for up to 3 weeks. Defrost still wrapped at room temperature. Unwrap and warm in a 350°F oven for 10 minutes before serving.

Fresh Fruit Scones

Add 1 loosely packed cup chopped fresh fruit to the flour mixture (see Note). Fresh peeled peaches, strawberries, raspberries, cherries, and blueberries are all delicious. Gently fold into the cream mixture. If the fruit is very juicy, decrease the cream to ½ cup. Proceed as directed.

Note: If using fruit that is exceptionally tender, such as raspberries or blackberries, lay them out in a single layer on a cookie sheet and freeze them for at least 1 hour before adding them to the flour mixture.

Dried Fruit Scones

Add ½ cup chopped dried fruit (cut into ¼-inch pieces) to the cream mixture. Raisins, currants, cherries, apricots, strawberries, etc., make wonderful dried fruit add-ins. Fold into the flour mixture. Proceed as directed.

GUINNESS GINGERBREAD

Gingerbread! I grew up making it for my Dad, it was one of his favorites at teatime on Sunday evenings. I'd whip cream with vanilla and just a little bit of sugar till it just held itself up, then serve a dollop of cream on top of the still-warm gingerbread. It would just start to get melty by the time we took our first bites.

Truthfully, back then the gingerbread was from a box, though it really was very good! My Guinness Gingerbread is a bit more sophisticated, with dark chocolaty stout, rich cocoa powder, and lots of spices—even a bit of hot white pepper.

Makes one 9-inch cake

⅔ cup Guinness stout
2 cups all-purpose flour
2 tablespoons best-quality unsweetened Dutch-process cocoa
  powder
1¼ teaspoons baking soda
2¼ teaspoons ground ginger
¼ teaspoon freshly ground white pepper
1 teaspoon ground cinnamon
2 large eggs
½ cup granulated sugar
⅓ cup firmly packed dark brown sugar
⅔ cup molasses
¾ cup vegetable or canola oil

BEFORE YOU START

Position a rack in the center of your oven. Preheat the oven to 350°F. Lightly butter and flour a 9 × 9 × 2-inch square cake pan.

1. In a medium saucepan, bring the beer to a simmer and remove from the heat.

2. Sift together the flour, cocoa powder, baking soda, ginger, white pepper, and cinnamon into a medium bowl.

3. In a large bowl, whisk the eggs, granulated sugar, brown sugar, and molasses until smooth. Whisk in the oil to combine. Whisk in the dry ingredients in three batches,

alternating with the beer. (Dry, beer, dry, beer, dry.) Mix until *just* combined. Do not overmix.

4. Pour the batter into the prepared cake pan. Bake for 50 to 60 minutes, or until a wooden skewer inserted into the center comes out clean. Remove to a wire rack to cool.

The gingerbread is best when served warm from the pan with freshly whipped cream (page 131). It keeps well wrapped in plastic wrap at room temperature for up to 3 days, or refrigerated for up to 1 week.

MOM'S BANANA APPLE BREAD

This is my spin on an old classic—banana bread that is outstanding even without the addition of the brown sugar apples. You can also add walnuts, pecans, raisins, or currants to the plain banana bread to create your own classic. Be sure to use super-ripe bananas, the blacker the better (see Pro tip)! **Makes 1½-quart loaf pan**

FOR THE APPLES
2 tablespoons unsalted butter
3 tablespoons firmly packed dark brown sugar
2 Granny Smith apples, peeled, cored, and cut into ½-inch
  pieces
½ teaspoon ground cinnamon
½ teaspoon pure vanilla extract

FOR THE BANANA BREAD
2 cups all-purpose flour
1 teaspoon baking soda
½ teaspoon ground cinnamon
¼ teaspoon ground cloves
¼ teaspoon freshly ground nutmeg
½ teaspoon kosher salt
8 tablespoons (1 stick) unsalted butter
1 cup granulated sugar
2 large eggs
¼ cup fresh orange juice
1 teaspoon pure vanilla extract
1¼ cups very ripe mashed bananas (2 to 3)

BEFORE YOU START

Position a rack in the center of your oven and preheat the oven to 350°F. Lightly butter and flour a 1½-quart loaf pan.

TO MAKE THE APPLES

Preheat a medium skillet over medium-high heat. Add the butter and brown sugar and heat until bubbling. Add the apples and cinnamon and sauté until golden and tender, about 5 minutes. Stir in the vanilla. Remove from the heat and set aside to cool.

TO MAKE THE BANANA BREAD

1. In a medium bowl, whisk together the flour, baking soda, cinnamon, cloves, nutmeg, and salt.

2. In the bowl of an electric mixer fitted with the paddle attachment, cream the butter and sugar until light and fluffy, 1 to 2 minutes. Add the eggs, one at a time, mixing well after each addition. Scrape down the sides of the bowl.

3. In a small bowl, combine the orange juice and vanilla.

4. Add the flour mixture to the butter mixture in three batches, alternating with the orange juice mixture, mixing well after each addition. Scrape down the sides of the bowl after each flour addition. Stir in the mashed bananas until combined. Then stir in the reserved apples.

5. Pour the batter into the prepared loaf pan. Bake for 55 to 60 minutes, or until a wooden skewer inserted into the center comes out clean. Remove to a wire rack to cool for 20 minutes before unmolding onto the rack to cool further.

Serve slightly warm or at room temperature. The banana bread keeps well wrapped in plastic wrap at room temperature for up to 3 days. For longer storage, freeze well wrapped in plastic wrap and then aluminum foil for up to 3 weeks. Defrost still wrapped at room temperature.

PRO TIP: If your bananas are black before you are ready to bake, peel them, puree them, and store them in an airtight plastic container in your freezer. You can add more to the container whenever you like; the bananas keep a very long time. When you are ready to bake, just defrost them in the container and get on with it.

PRETTY SLICK: If after a few days, the banana bread starts to get dry, toast a slice and spread some soft butter on top. It's great this way with your morning coffee or afternoon tea.

WHOLE ORANGE–POPPY SEED CAKE

I taught this recipe to a group of beginning pastry students at the French Culinary Institute. It's one of my favorite cakes, and they thought it was so cool that I use the entire orange. It's not too sweet, just really, really moist and absolutely delicious.

Makes 1½-quart loaf pan

FOR THE CAKE
1 whole orange, washed well
1 cup sugar
3 large eggs
12 tablespoons (1½ sticks) unsalted butter, melted
1½ cups all-purpose flour
2¼ teaspoons baking powder
¾ teaspoon kosher salt
1 tablespoon poppy seeds

FOR THE GLAZE
2 tablespoons fresh orange juice
2 tablespoons fresh lemon juice
¼ cup sugar

BEFORE YOU START

Position a rack in the center of your oven. Preheat the oven to 350°F. Lightly butter and flour a 1½-quart loaf pan.

1. Using a sharp knife, remove the little green stem from the orange skin. Cut the orange into 8 pieces.

2. In the bowl of a food processor fitted with the metal blade, pulse the orange pieces (skin and all!) and ½ cup of the sugar until pureed, scraping down the sides of the bowl as needed, so that no large orange skin pieces remain.

3. In a large mixing bowl, whisk together the eggs and the remaining ½ cup sugar until smooth. Stir in the orange pulp. Whisk in the melted butter to combine.

4. In a separate bowl, whisk together the flour, baking powder, salt, and poppy seeds to combine. Sprinkle over the orange mixture and, using a rubber spatula, gently fold until just combined.

5. Pour the batter into the prepared loaf pan. Bake for 50 to 60 minutes, rotating the pan halfway through baking. The cake is done when a wooden skewer inserted into the center comes out clean. Remove to a wire rack and cool for 20 minutes before unmolding the cake onto the rack for glazing.

6. *For the glaze:* In a small saucepan, combine the orange juice, lemon juice, and sugar at a high simmer. Simmer for 2 to 3 minutes, or until reduced by half.

7. Using a pastry brush, brush the hot glaze all over the cake while it is still warm.

The cake keeps tightly wrapped in plastic wrap at room temperature for 2 days. For longer storage, wrap in plastic wrap and refrigerate for up to 5 days, or freeze well wrapped in plastic wrap and then aluminum foil for up to 3 weeks. Defrost still wrapped at room temperature.

Lemon-Poppy Seed Cake

Use 1½ lemons instead of the whole orange and an additional 2 tablespoons sugar in the batter. For a lemon glaze, combine ¼ cup fresh lemon juice with ¼ cup sugar. Proceed as directed.

GOLDEN ALMOND FRUITCAKE

This recipe won the 2006 Marzipandemonium contest sponsored by the Almond Board of California, which I think is pretty darn impressive considering how many people feel about fruitcake. For some reason, there seems to be a stigma against fruitcakes. So, feel free to rename this delicious cake (Golden Almond Tea Bread?) if you find yourself having to convince your friends to try it. When I make it over the holidays at Sweet Melissa's, I have to put lots of free samples out on the counter for my customers to taste. Once they taste it, they often buy more than one.

 It is delicious and easy. We use a combination of dried apricots, golden raisins, pineapple, and sour cherries. Any dried fruits can be substituted (like dried strawberries and raspberries, for example), but omitting the marzipan would be a sin.

Makes one loaf fruitcake

FOR THE CAKE
1 cup chopped dried fruit (¼- to ½-inch pieces)
¼ cup brandy, apple juice, or orange juice
8 tablespoons (1 stick) unsalted butter, softened
½ cup granulated sugar
⅓ cup firmly packed light brown sugar
1 teaspoon freshly grated lemon zest
3 large eggs
½ teaspoon almond extract
1 teaspoon pure vanilla extract
⅓ cup almond flour or ½ cup sliced blanched almonds
1 cup all-purpose flour
½ teaspoon baking soda
½ teaspoon ground cardamom
¼ teaspoon freshly ground nutmeg
¼ teaspoon kosher salt
½ cup whole natural almonds, coarsely chopped
¼ cup (2.5 ounces) marzipan, cut into ¼- to ½-inch pieces and
 frozen

FOR THE GLAZE
¼ cup brandy, apple juice, or orange juice
3 tablespoons sugar

PRO TIP: To make your own almond flour for this recipe, in a food processor pulse ½ cup sliced blanched almonds with ¼ cup of the granulated sugar called for in the recipe until it becomes a coarse flour texture. The remaining ¼ cup of sugar should be added to the butter for creaming.

BEFORE YOU START

Position a rack in the center of your oven. Preheat the oven to 350°F. Lightly butter and flour a 1½-quart loaf pan.

1. In a medium saucepan over very low heat, heat the dried fruit and brandy, stirring occasionally. When the mixture comes to a simmer, remove from the heat and cover (allowing the fruit to absorb the brandy), stirring occasionally.

2. In the bowl of an electric mixer fitted with the paddle attachment, cream the butter, sugars, and zest until light and fluffy, 3 to 5 minutes. Add the eggs, one at a time, mixing well after each addition. Scrape down the sides of the bowl. Add the almond extract and vanilla. Mix until combined. (At this stage, the mixture will appear slightly broken.)

3. If using the sliced blanched almonds, in a food processor fitted with the metal blade, pulse grind the almonds until a very fine flour (as fine as you can get). In a medium bowl, whisk together the almond flour, all-purpose flour, baking soda, cardamom, nutmeg, and salt.

4. On low speed, add the flour mixture to the butter mixture in two batches, mixing until just combined after each addition. Scrape down the sides of the bowl. Using a rubber spatula, fold in the dried fruits along with their soaking liquid. Fold in two-thirds of the chopped almonds and the frozen marzipan (it's easy to forget this because it's in the freezer).

5. Pour the batter into the prepared loaf pan and sprinkle the remaining chopped almonds on top. Bake for 25 minutes, then rotate the pan and reduce the oven temperature to 325°F. Bake for an additional 30 to 35 minutes, or until a wooden skewer inserted into the center comes out clean. (Be careful when testing with the wooden skewer. You could poke into a piece of marzipan, which will look like raw cake batter on the skewer, so test the loaf in a few different spots.) Remove to a wire rack to cool for 20 minutes before unmolding the cake onto the rack for glazing.

6. *For the glaze:* Warm the brandy with the sugar until the sugar dissolves (it's easiest to do this in the microwave, 30 seconds at a time).

7 Using a pastry brush, brush the glaze over the fruitcake while it is still warm. You will not need all of the glaze, but use as much as you like. Glaze the cake at least once, but if you want more, simply wait for each layer to soak in before you glaze again. The more you glaze, the boozier your fruitcake will be. Let cool to room temperature.

This cake keeps very well tightly wrapped in plastic wrap at room temperature for 2 days. For longer storage, wrap in plastic wrap and refrigerate for 5 days, or freeze well wrapped in plastic wrap and then aluminum foil for up to 3 weeks. Defrost still wrapped at room temperature.

SWEET POTATO BREAD WITH CINNAMON-RUM-ORANGE GLAZE

Every Friday Jessie, one of my top bakers at Sweet Melissa's, makes quick breads and loaf cakes for those customers getting ready to go out of town for the weekend. They stop in on their way out to the Hamptons on Long Island or the Jersey Shore and pick up a stash of Sweet Melissa's treats to nibble on. I love the thought of my cakes and cookies in their beautiful kitchens with ocean views.

This quick bread has "home sweet home" written all over it. One of the many things I like about this recipe, which is based on a recipe by my all-time favorite pastry chef, Andrea Lekberg, is that it is so inexpensive to make and is one of the best things you'll ever eat.

The staff at Sweet Melissa's goes crazy for sweet potato bread. We make an extra one just for slicing so we can all get our fill (which is very good for morale!).

Makes one Bundt pan

FOR THE BREAD
Two 15-ounce cans sweet potatoes, drained
2 cups sugar
⅔ cup vegetable or canola oil
2 large eggs
2 cups all-purpose flour
¾ teaspoon baking soda
½ teaspoon baking powder
¾ teaspoon ground cinnamon
½ teaspoon ground cloves
½ teaspoon freshly ground nutmeg
¾ teaspoon kosher salt
⅔ cup pecans, coarsely chopped

FOR THE CINNAMON-RUM-ORANGE GLAZE
¼ cup fresh orange juice
¼ cup rum
½ cup sugar
2 cinnamon sticks

BEFORE YOU START

Position a rack in the center of your oven. Preheat the oven to 350°F. Butter and flour a 10-cup Bundt pan.

1. In the bowl of an electric mixer fitted with the paddle attachment on low speed, mash the sweet potatoes until smooth (this will make about 2 cups). Add the sugar and oil and mix to combine. Add the eggs, one at a time, mixing well after each addition. Scrape down the sides of the bowl.

2. In a separate bowl, whisk together the flour, baking soda, baking powder, cinnamon, cloves,nutmeg, and salt. Add the flour mixture into the sweet potato mixture in three batches, mixing well after each addition. Scrape down the sides of the bowl. Do not overmix. Stir in the pecans.

3. Pour the batter into the prepared Bundt pan. Spin the pan to level the batter. Bake for about 1 hour and 10 minutes, or until a wooden skewer inserted into the center comes out clean. Remove to a wire rack to cool for 20 minutes before inverting onto the rack for glazing.

4. *For the glaze:* Combine the orange juice, rum, sugar, and cinnamon sticks in a small nonreactive saucepan. Bring to a simmer over low heat and reduce by half. Remove from the heat and set aside to cool slightly before glazing.

5. Using a pastry brush, brush the glaze generously over the still-warm bread. Wait for 10 minutes and glaze again.

Serve at room temperature. Sweet potato bread keeps well wrapped in plastic wrap at room temperature for up to 3 days. For longer storage, freeze wrapped in plastic wrap and then in aluminum foil for up to 3 weeks. Defrost still wrapped at room temperature.

MOM'S FRENCH PANCAKES

My Mom says:

If the Murphys love any particular meal, it is breakfast, and the very favorite choice for a special Sunday breakfast is French pancakes. They were dubbed French pancakes by "Old Grandma," who came to America from Latvia in the early part of the twentieth century. Old Grandma made them for her grandson, Melissa's father, Jim, when he was a boy.

The trick, Old Grandma explained, was not in the recipe, but in the cooking. It took a special skill and a special pan to make these delicacies just right.

When Melissa became a student at the French Culinary Institute, she quickly informed me that these pancakes were in fact crepes, and a standby in French cooking. We eat them rolled up with homemade peach or strawberry preserves spread inside down the middle, and they disappear before I can finish cooking them! My grown sons now make them for their own families, and I always know when they'll be served. Before they make the batter, they have to call their mother: "Mom can you tell me how to make those French pancakes again?" **Makes about twenty 12-inch pancakes**

1½ cups whole milk
4 large eggs
1 teaspoon canola oil or melted butter, plus more for the skillet
1 cup all-purpose flour
1 teaspoon sugar
¼ teaspoon kosher salt

1. In a blender, combine the milk, eggs, and oil and pulse for a few seconds to blend. Add the flour, sugar, and salt and pulse again until the batter is smooth. Do not overmix. The batter should be the consistency of heavy cream. For the best results, let it rest covered in the refrigerator for at least 1 hour or overnight before using.

2. Preheat a 12-inch skillet (a seasoned cast-iron one works well, or a crepe pan, if you have one). Rub the pan with a few drops of oil. Repeat between pancakes if the skillet looks dry. When the skillet is hot (drop a tiny dot of batter on the skillet to check—if it sizzles, it's ready), pour about ¼ cup of batter onto the pan, then quickly pick up the pan and swirl the batter around, aiming for a round shape (this takes practice, but is not *that* difficult).

3. When the surface of the crepe appears dry, use an angled offset spatula to loosen it around the edges (I have used a metal cake server in a pinch). Quickly slip the spatula under the crepe, flip it, and remove it from the pan almost immediately. Repeat as desired. (You can freeze unused batter in an airtight container for up to 1 month. Whisk together until smooth once defrosted.)

Serve warm filled with jam, fresh fruit, ice cream, or whipped cream (page 131) and sprinkle with confectioners' sugar. Enjoy! Crepes can be frozen between layers of wax paper and wrapped in plastic wrap and then in aluminum foil for up to 3 weeks. Defrost still wrapped at room temperature.

CARAMEL APPLE TURNOVERS WITH SWEET RICOTTA FILLING

This recipe is one that I created when the French Culinary Institute asked me to write a recipe utilizing puff pastry. Now, I took the pastry course, so I know they already have the beautiful mille-feuille (or French Napoleon), the bourdelots (or fancy baked apple), and palmiers (crispy, caramelized sugar "angel wings"). As I am forever trying to Americanize their curriculum (mastering pie dough will be a prerequisite to graduating), I thought this rustic yet elegant turnover would be a fun way to put my own touch on the classic dough. **Makes 4 turnovers**

FOR THE CARAMEL APPLE FILLING
¼ cup sugar
¼ cup water
2 Granny Smith apples, peeled, cored, and cut into ¼-inch
  pieces
Pinch salt

FOR THE SWEET RICOTTA FILLING
½ cup ricotta, drained overnight (see Note)
1 large egg yolk
2 tablespoons sugar
1 tablespoon all-purpose flour
½ teaspoon pure vanilla extract
⅛ teaspoon kosher salt
½ teaspoon freshly grated orange zest

FOR ASSEMBLING THE TURNOVERS
1 large egg
2 tablespoons heavy cream or whole milk
½ teaspoon ground cinnamon
3 tablespoons sugar
One 12-inch square puff pastry, ¼-inch thick, chilled

BEFORE YOU START

Position a rack in the center of your oven. Preheat the oven to 375°F.

TO MAKE THE CARAMEL APPLE FILLING

1. In a small heavy-bottomed saucepan over low heat, heat the sugar and 2 table-spoons of the water until amber.

2. Add the apples and stir to combine. Continue to cook over low heat, stirring occasionally to prevent burning. Once the apples begin to soften, add the remaining 2 tablespoons water and the salt and cook until they are a tender, chunky sauce consistency. Set aside to cool. (The caramel apple filling can be made up to 3 days ahead and kept in an airtight container in the refrigerator.)

TO MAKE THE SWEET RICOTTA FILLING

In a medium bowl, combine the ricotta, egg yolk, sugar, flour, vanilla, salt, and zest and whisk until smooth. Refrigerate until ready to use. (The sweet ricotta filling can be made up to 3 days ahead and kept in an airtight container in the refrigerator.)

TO ASSEMBLE THE TURNOVERS

1. In a small bowl, combine the egg and heavy cream with a fork. Set aside. This is your egg wash.

2. In another small bowl, combine the cinnamon with the sugar. Set aside. This is your cinnamon sugar.

3. Place the chilled puff pastry on a lightly floured board. With a sharp knife, cut the pastry into four 6-inch squares. Place one-quarter of the ricotta filling just off center on each of the 4 squares. Place one-quarter of the caramel apple filling on top of the ricotta.

4. Using a pastry brush, brush the egg wash around the edges of each square. Fold each pastry in half, corner to corner, to form 4 triangles. Gently press together the washed edges of the turnover to seal, and gently pat down each mound of filling so that it fills the pocket of each triangle. Chill the pastries until firm. (The pastries may be assembled to this point and frozen wrapped in plastic wrap and aluminum foil for up to 3 weeks.)

5. Using the pastry brush, brush the tops of the turnovers with the remaining egg wash and sprinkle generously with the cinnamon sugar. Cut three steam vents in the top of each turnover. Bake for 45 minutes, or until deep golden brown. Remove to a wire rack to cool.

The turnovers are best served warm the day they are made.

Note: To drain the cheese, line a strainer with one to two layers of cheesecloth. Set over a deep bowl, making sure the strainer does not touch the bottom of the bowl. Place the ricotta in the lined strainer. Lay a sheet of plastic wrap over the top of the cheese and place a plate on top of the plastic wrap to act as a weight on the cheese.

PRO TIP: You can quadruple the caramel apple filling for a delicious apple-sauce, great with a roast pork or turkey dinner, or atop potato pancakes!

LEMON WALNUT–SOUR CREAM POUND CAKE

This is one of my favorite Friday-morning loaf cakes to make for my shop. It has a beautiful rise and a nice golden color. The fresh lemon juice and zest in the cake give lots of flavor, and the sour cream in the batter keeps the cake nice and moist.

Makes one pound cake

FOR THE CAKE
8 tablespoons (1 stick) unsalted butter, softened
¼ cup vegetable shortening
1½ cups sugar
2 teaspoons freshly grated lemon zest
2 tablespoons fresh lemon juice
¼ teaspoon almond extract
1 teaspoon pure vanilla extract
3 large eggs
1½ cups all-purpose flour
¼ teaspoon baking powder
½ teaspoon kosher salt
½ cup sour cream
1 cup walnuts, coarsely chopped

FOR THE GLAZE
¼ cup sugar
¼ cup fresh lemon juice

BEFORE YOU START

Position a rack in the center of your oven. Preheat the oven to 350°F. Butter and flour a 1½-quart loaf pan.

1. In the bowl of an electric mixer fitted with the paddle attachment, cream the butter, shortening, sugar, and zest, 3 to 5 minutes. Add the lemon juice, almond extract, and vanilla and mix to combine. Add the eggs, one at a time, mixing well after each addition. Scrape down the sides of the bowl.

2. In a separate bowl, whisk together the flour, baking powder, and salt. Add the flour mixture to the batter in two batches, alternating with the sour cream. Do not overmix. Scrape down the sides of the bowl. Gently fold in the walnuts, saving some to sprinkle on top.

3. Bake for 1 hour and 15 minutes to 1 hour and 30 minutes, or until a wooden skewer inserted into the center comes out clean. Remove to a wire rack to cool for 20 minutes before inverting onto a rack for glazing.

4. *For the glaze:* In a small saucepan, combine the sugar and lemon juice and heat to a high simmer. Simmer for 2 to 3 minutes, or until reduced by half.

5. Using a pastry brush, brush the hot glaze on the still-warm unmolded cake. Brush again, if desired, after 10 minutes. Let cool before slicing.

The pound cake keeps well wrapped in plastic wrap for 3 to 4 days at room temperature. For longer storage, freeze well wrapped in plastic wrap and then aluminum foil for up to 1 month. Defrost still wrapped at room temperature.

SWEET PLUM CLAFOUTIS WITH ALMONDS

This is an easy dish, perfect for breakfast and brunch, and even as a light dessert. If you are using a seasoned cast-iron skillet, start the clafoutis on the stove, finish it in the oven, and then serve it in the skillet. Otherwise, cook the plums in a sauté or frying pan, transfer the cooked fruit to any lightly buttered ovenproof baking dish, pour the batter over, and finish in the oven.

Makes 8 to 10 servings

FOR THE CLAFOUTIS
6 large eggs
¾ cup sugar
⅓ cup all-purpose flour
1 tablespoon freshly grated orange zest
½ teaspoon almond extract
¾ cup heavy cream
¾ cup whole milk
3 tablespoons sliced blanched almonds
Confectioners' sugar, for dusting

FOR THE PLUMS
3 tablespoons unsalted butter
¼ cup sugar
¼ teaspoon ground cinnamon
10 small Italian plums (or fresh prunes) or 5 medium black
  plums, sliced into eighths

BEFORE YOU START

Position a rack in the center of your oven. Preheat the oven to 350°F.

TO MAKE THE BATTER

In a medium bowl, whisk together the eggs, sugar, flour, zest, almond extract, heavy cream, and milk until smooth.

TO MAKE THE PLUMS

In a 10-inch cast-iron skillet set over medium heat, melt the butter. Stir in the sugar and cinnamon and cook until just bubbly. Stir in the plums and sauté until tender, but not yet losing their skins, stirring gently all the while. Remove from the heat.

TO COMPLETE THE CLAFOUTIS

When the plums have stopped bubbling, gently stir in the batter. Sprinkle the almonds around the outside edge of the pan. Bake for 30 minutes or until pouffed and golden. Sprinkle the edges with confectioners' sugar.

The clafoutis is best eaten the day it is made. Serve warm cut into wedges and topped with a dollop of sweetened crème fraîche or sour cream.

HOT PEPPER GINGERBREAD MUFFINS WITH ORANGE MAPLE BUTTER

I know this is a long list of ingredients, and you couldn't possibly follow this recipe on a groggy Sunday morning (well, I can't anyway). Luckily, you can make these muffins the night before; the batter rises even better after it rests. Be sure to fill the muffin cups all the way. Serve these spicy muffins warm with the easy orange maple butter. They will really awaken your senses and put you in a holiday mood when it's cold and blustery outside.

Makes 12 muffins

FOR THE MUFFINS
1¾ cups all-purpose flour
1¼ teaspoons baking soda
¼ teaspoon kosher salt
2½ teaspoons ground ginger
¼ teaspoon powdered dry mustard
1 teaspoon ground cinnamon
½ teaspoon ground cloves
¼ teaspoon freshly ground black pepper
⅛ teaspoon freshly ground white pepper
⅛ teaspoon ground cayenne pepper
½ teaspoon ground cardamom
2 large eggs
½ cup firmly packed dark brown sugar
¼ cup granulated sugar
⅓ cup vegetable or canola oil
½ cup molasses
3 tablespoons freshly grated gingerroot
⅔ cup strong boiling hot coffee

FOR THE ORANGE MAPLE BUTTER
8 tablespoons (1 stick) unsalted butter, at room temperature
2 teaspoons freshly grated orange zest
2 tablespoons pure maple syrup
⅛ teaspoon fine salt

BEFORE YOU START

Position a rack in the center of your oven. Preheat the oven to 350°F. Line a standard 12-cup muffin tin with muffin papers (or butter and flour the cups or spray with nonstick vegetable cooking spray).

TO MAKE THE MUFFINS

1. In a medium bowl, whisk together the flour, baking soda, salt, ginger, dry mustard, cinnamon, cloves, black pepper, white pepper, cayenne, and cardamom.

2. In the bowl of an electric mixer fitted with the whip attachment, beat the eggs, brown sugar, and granulated sugar until thick. In a slow, steady stream, add the oil and molasses. Stir in the ginger.

3. On medium speed, add the flour mixture in three batches, alternating with the hot coffee and mixing well after each addition. Scrape down the sides of the bowl.

4. Pour the muffin batter into the prepared muffin cups. (If you like, refrigerate over-night at this point.) Bake for 30 to 35 minutes, or until a skewer inserted into the center comes out clean. Remove to a wire rack to cool. Sprinkle with confectioners' sugar.

TO MAKE THE BUTTER

In a medium bowl, whisk together the butter, zest, maple syrup, and salt until smooth. Serve at room temperature.

Serve the muffins with the orange maple butter. The butter keeps refrigerated in an airtight container for up to 1 week. Allow it to soften to room temperature before serving. When soft, the butter may be rewhipped, if necessary.

CHERRY ALMOND GRANOLA

When I was a child, my best friend, Adrienne, and I raised bunnies and ruled our 4-H club, the Rabbit Raisers. She and I were inseparable, attached at the hip, and got into all kinds of mischief as we grew up together.

When I smell this granola baking, it reminds me of the quiet peacefulness of Adrienne's home. Her mom, Cindy, used to bake granola in a big Dutch oven at a very low temperature. Cindy and her husband, Peter, would take turns stirring it throughout the day. What strikes me now is how much food can create sensory memories for us all. As Cindy was baking the granola, I'm sure she enjoyed it well enough—but did she realize that she was creating a wonderful memory that would last the rest of my life?

This granola has quite a following at Sweet Melissa's. It's not Cindy's recipe—I never did get that—but it smells like her recipe. My customers love the variety of flakes, the dried cherries, and the toasted almonds. It's not too sweet as it's made with pure maple syrup and honey.

This recipe easily doubles or triples. Just be sure to save some for Granola Breakfast Cookies (see page 36).

Makes 4 quarts granola

5 cups rolled oats
3 cups rye flakes (see Note)
1 cup unsalted shelled sunflower seeds
1 cup roasted shelled pumpkin seeds
1 cup whole natural almonds
½ cup dry milk powder
½ cup canola or vegetable oil
¾ cup clover honey
¾ cup pure maple syrup
1 teaspoon ground cinnamon
¼ teaspoon freshly ground nutmeg
¼ teaspoon ground cloves
¼ teaspoon ground allspice
¼ teaspoon ground ginger
1 cup dried currants
1 cup dried cherries
1 cup golden raisins

BEFORE YOU START

Position a rack in the bottom and top thirds of your oven. Preheat the oven to 250°F. Line two cookie sheets with parchment paper or aluminum foil.

1. In a very large bowl, combine the oats, rye flakes, sunflower and pumpkin seeds, almonds, and dry milk powder.

2. In a medium saucepan over medium-low heat, whisk together the oil, honey, maple syrup, cinnamon, nutmeg, cloves, allspice, and ginger and bring to a simmer, 3 to 4 minutes.

3. Pour the hot mixture over the oat mixture, and mix well to combine.

4. Divide the granola equally between the prepared cookie sheets, spreading it evenly into a single layer. Bake for 1½ to 2 hours, stirring every 15 minutes, until golden. Remove to a wire rack to cool completely.

5. Break up the granola into a bowl. Add the currants, cherries, and raisins and mix thoroughly.

The granola keeps in an airtight container at room temperature and in the refrigerator for up to 1 month.

Note: Rye flakes are similar to rolled oats and can be used in much the same way. You can find them at natural foods stores.

GRANOLA BREAKFAST COOKIES

These are a perfect on-the-go morning snack—full of honey goodness.

Makes 2 dozen cookies

6 tablespoons unsalted butter, melted
½ cup clover honey
¼ cup molasses
1 large egg
1¾ cups whole wheat flour
¼ teaspoon kosher salt
½ teaspoon ground cinnamon
1¼ teaspoons baking soda
1½ cups Cherry Almond Granola (page 34)

BEFORE YOU START

Position a rack in the center of your oven. Preheat the oven to 350°F. Line two cookie sheets with parchment paper or aluminum foil.

1. In a large bowl, whisk together the butter, honey, and molasses until smooth. Add the egg and whisk until incorporated.

2. In a separate bowl, whisk together the flour, salt, cinnamon, and baking soda.

3. Add the flour mixture to the honey mixture all at once and stir until combined. Stir in the granola. (At this point, the dough can be stored in an airtight container in the freezer for up to 1 month.)

4. Drop the batter 2 inches apart by rounded tablespoonfuls onto the prepared cookie sheets (12 on each sheet). Bake for 12 to 13 minutes, or until golden around the edges. Do not overbake. The cookies should be nice and chewy when cool. Remove to a rack to cool on the sheets for 10 minutes before transferring to the rack.

The cookies will keep layered between wax paper in an airtight container at room temperature for 4 days, or frozen for up to 3 weeks.

IRISH SODA BREAD

Irish soda bread is so yummy it's a shame we tend to make it only once a year. I developed this recipe to be so easy that there is just no excuse not to make it every day! (Just kidding.) Of course this bread is delicious with all kinds of boiled meat dinners, not just corned beef. My favorite way to eat it? Toasted, spread with butter and strawberry jam, served alongside a cup of hot tea.

Makes one 3-pound loaf or two 1½-pound loaves soda bread

½ cup golden raisins
½ cup dried black currants
3 cups all-purpose flour
1 tablespoon baking powder
1 teaspoon baking soda
⅓ cup sugar
1½ teaspoon kosher salt
⅛ teaspoon ground cloves
6 tablespoons cold unsalted butter, cut into ¼-inch pieces
2 tablespoons caraway seeds (optional)
1 large egg
1 cup buttermilk

BEFORE YOU START

Position a rack in the center of your oven. Preheat the oven to 350°F. Line a baking sheet with parchment paper or aluminum foil.

1. In a medium bowl, combine the raisins and currants. Pour boiling water over to cover and set aside to reconstitute.

2. In the bowl of an electric mixer fitted with the paddle attachment, combine the flour, baking powder, baking soda, sugar, salt, and cloves. Add the cold butter pieces and mix on low speed until the butter is the size of small peas. Add the caraway seeds, if using, and mix to blend.

3. In a separate bowl, whisk together the egg and buttermilk.

4. Add the buttermilk mixture to the flour mixture and mix on low speed until just combined. Be sure to scrape down the sides and the bottom of the bowl to combine thoroughly. Do not overmix.

5. Drain the raisins and currants thoroughly. Add them to the dough and mix on low speed for 20 seconds.

6. Turn the dough out onto a lightly floured work surface. Knead the dough gently, until the ingredients are fully incorporated. Using a little flour if needed, form the dough into one large round—or divide it in half to form two small rounds.

7. Place the round (rounds) on the prepared baking sheet. Using a sharp knife, cut the traditional "X" cutting about 1½ inches deep into the top. Bake for 20 minutes, reduce the oven temperature to 325°F, and bake for an additional 20 minutes for the large loaf, or 10 minutes for the smaller loaves. The loaves will be golden, and a wooden skewer inserted into the center will come out clean. Remove to a wire rack to cool.

Irish soda bread is best eaten the day it is made, but it can be tightly wrapped in plastic wrap and kept at room temperature for 2 days. For longer storage, wrap in plastic wrap and refrigerate for up to 5 days, or freeze well wrapped in plastic wrap and then aluminum foil for up to 3 weeks. Defrost still wrapped at room temperature.

STICKY BUNS WITH TOASTED ALMONDS

These sticky buns are out of this world—well worth the little bit of time and effort it takes to make them. In this recipe, I've shown you how to break it up into two steps: Make and roll the dough the night before you want to serve the sticky buns. In the morning you just let them have their final rise and bake. Come on, you can do that.

Makes 12 buns

FOR THE DOUGH
1 large egg yolk
1 cup whole milk
1 teaspoon pure vanilla extract
Zest of 1 orange
2½ to 2¾ cups all-purpose flour
2 tablespoons unsalted butter, softened
2¼ teaspoons (1 package) active dry yeast
1½ teaspoons kosher salt
¼ cup sugar

FOR THE STICKY SAUCE
½ pound (2 sticks) unsalted butter
¾ cup firmly packed light brown sugar
½ cup pure maple syrup
1½ teaspoons ground cinnamon

FOR THE EGG WASH
1 large egg
2 tablespoons whole milk or heavy cream

FOR THE CINNAMON SUGAR
1 tablespoon plus 1½ teaspoons freshly ground cinnamon
½ cup sugar

FOR FINISHING
1 cup whole natural almonds, lightly toasted and coarsely
  chopped

TO MAKE THE DOUGH (FIRST RISE)

1. In the bowl of an electric mixer fitted with the whip attachment, combine the egg yolk, milk, vanilla, zest, and one-third of the flour. Mix on medium speed until it is a smooth paste. Add the butter in pieces and mix to combine.

2. Change the mixer attachment to the dough hook. Add the remaining flour, the yeast, salt, and sugar and mix on low speed to combine. Increase the speed to medium and beat for 10 to 15 minutes, or until the dough forms a ball and is no longer sticking to the sides of the bowl. The dough should be nice and elastic. If it is very sticky, slowly add up to ½ cup more flour.

3. Place the dough in a lightly greased bowl and cover with plastic wrap. Set aside in a warm place to rise until doubled in volume, 1½ to 2 hours.

TO MAKE THE STICKY SAUCE

1. Generously butter a 9 × 13-inch baking pan.

2. In a medium saucepan, combine the butter, brown sugar, maple syrup, and cinnamon, stirring until it reaches a rolling boil.

3. Remove from the heat and pour into the prepared pan. Set aside to cool.

TO MAKE THE DOUGH (SECOND RISE)

1. When the dough has doubled in volume, punch it down and turn it out onto a lightly floured work surface. Roll out the dough into a rectangle that is 12 inches wide by 18 inches long.

2. *For the egg wash:* In a small bowl, using a fork, whisk together the egg and milk. Using a pastry brush, brush it over the surface of the dough.

3. *For the cinnamon sugar:* In a small bowl, combine the cinnamon and sugar. Sprinkle over the dough, leaving unsugared the bottom 1 inch of one long side of the rectangle.

4. Starting at the top edge of the rectangle, roll the dough toward you jelly-roll style and pinch the bottom seam closed. Slice the roll into 12 pieces approximately 1½ inches thick, and place them cut side up about 2 inches apart on top of the sticky sauce in the pan. Spray the buns lightly with nonstick vegetable cooking spray and cover with plastic wrap (or lightly butter one side of the plastic wrap). Refrigerate overnight.

TO COMPLETE THE BUNS

1. When you are ready for the final rise, remove the buns from the refrigerator. Bring about 3 quarts of water to a boil. Place an empty roasting pan large enough to hold the water on the bottom of your cold oven. Pour the boiling water into the pan.

2. Remove the plastic wrap from the buns. Position a rack in the center of your oven. Place the pan on the rack in the oven (do not turn it on!) and shut the door. The steam of the water will help the buns in their final rise. The buns will just about double in size in 30 to 45 minutes. (If your fridge is on a super-cold setting, the buns may take a little longer to rise. If they need more time, just boil some more water and refill the roasting pan.) When the buns have doubled in volume, remove them (and the roasting pan filled with water) from the oven.

3. Preheat the oven to 350°F.

4. Bake for 45 to 50 minutes, or until golden brown. Remove to a wire rack to cool for about 10 minutes. Using tongs, turn the buns over onto a serving dish. Pour the sticky sauce in the pan over the buns and sprinkle with the chopped almonds.

Cinnamon Buns

Prepare the dough as directed. Do not make the sticky sauce. Place the buns in a buttered 9 × 13-inch baking pan, proof in the oven, and bake (sans sauce). Remove to a wire rack to cool for about 10 minutes before spreading the top of each bun liberally with cream cheese frosting. My oh my!

For cream cheese frosting: In the bowl of an electric mixer fitted with the paddle attachment, mix together 3 ounces cream cheese, 1 tablespoon whole milk, and 1½ cups confectioners' sugar until smooth.

RAISED WAFFLES WITH WARM BROWN SUGAR BANANAS

This recipe combines the best of both breakfast and dessert—what a sweet warm way to welcome the day! The brown sugar bananas are a version of the classic bananas Foster and are also delicious served over ice cream. Better yet, for a really great dessert (or my kind of breakfast!), top the waffle with ice cream and the warm bananas for a treat reminiscent of the Belgian waffles we would snack on at the Jersey shore. This recipe is based on the original Fannie Farmer *recipe for raised waffles. The waffles will not be very fat as the texture is best when baked in a standard waffle iron as opposed to a Belgian waffle iron. To serve these for breakfast, start the waffle batter the night before.*

Makes 6 large waffles

FOR THE WAFFLES
½ cup warm water
2¼ teaspoons (1 package) active dry yeast
8 tablespoons (1 stick) unsalted butter, cut into pieces
2 cups whole milk
1 teaspoon kosher salt
1 teaspoon sugar
2 cups all-purpose flour
Pinch freshly ground nutmeg
2 large eggs
¼ teaspoon baking soda

FOR THE BROWN SUGAR BANANAS
4 tablespoons (½ stick) unsalted butter, at room temperature
¼ cup firmly packed light brown sugar
Pinch kosher salt
¼ cup light rum
2 ripe bananas, peeled and sliced
½ cup pure maple syrup

TO MAKE THE WAFFLES

1. In a large bowl, combine the warm water and yeast. Let stand for 5 minutes to dissolve and activate.

2. In a small saucepan over low heat, melt the butter. Stir in the milk; the butter mixture should be warm but not hot.

3. Add the butter mixture, salt, sugar, flour, and nutmeg to the yeast mixture. Using a wire whisk, beat until smooth.

4. Cover the bowl with plastic wrap, and let stand at room temperature for at least 8 hours or overnight.

5. When you are ready to cook the waffles, preheat the waffle iron (see Pro tip).

6. In a medium bowl, whisk together the eggs and baking soda and immediately whisk them into the batter. The batter will be very thin but smooth.

7. Spray the waffle iron with nonstick vegetable cooking spray. Cook the waffles according to the manufacturer's instructions.

TO MAKE THE BANANAS

1. Melt the butter in a large skillet. Add the brown sugar and salt, and stir over medium heat until melted and bubbling.

2. Remove from the heat and add the rum, then carefully return the pan to the heat. Be careful when you add the rum and return the pan to the heat. The rum is going to flame up, but don't worry, it'll go out momentarily. Once the flame is out, burn off the alcohol, about 30 seconds.

3. Add the sliced bananas and stir to coat. Add the maple syrup and bring just to bubbling.

4. Remove from the heat to cool slightly.

Serve the bananas warm over the waffles.

PRO TIP: I also like to preheat my oven to 200°F to keep the finished waffles warm until I'm ready to serve them.

GOING TO THE BAKERY

I USED TO GO to the bakery with my dad on Sunday mornings, and my mom would let me wear whatever dress I chose. (Sometimes my brothers would insist on coming along and ruin everything, and I had no choice but to tolerate them.) We would take everyone's orders before we left, and I'd repeat them to myself on the car ride there so as not to forget. At the bakery, everyone knew my name, although I was too shy to ask theirs. They were so friendly whenever we came in. I loved to go to the bakery.

After breakfast, my brothers and I took turns on who got first pick of the Boston creams (our favorite), and somehow my brothers would never remember when it was my turn to choose first. They would always trick me. They'd pick up the doughnuts and tease me and pretend they were interested in one certain doughnut. Of course, this

drove me mad, and I insisted that they give me that one. They'd finally give in, and I'd take a bite of my prize possession, waiting for that cream to explode in my mouth, only to find a piddly squirt inside! My brothers would fall over laughing when they saw the disappointment on my face. Little did I know that all along they'd been weighing the doughnuts to see how much cream they contained and then act as though they were "interested" in the lightest one!

Some things never change. I still love cream-filled doughnuts, and my brothers will forever tease me. But now when I make my cream-filled Bee Stings (page 47), I'm sure to fill all of them to the max, and then I eat whichever one I want. I guess they can have some, too.

BEE STINGS

I created my Bee Stings out of my love for doughnuts. Unfortunately, I don't have a fryer at the bakery kitchen, so I needed to figure out how to bake them. I love the resulting compromise: sweet and tender brioche-style buns filled with pastry cream and then dipped in honey caramel and sprinkled with toasted almonds. Mm-mm-mm-yummy.

Makes 12 buns

FOR THE PASTRY CREAM
1 recipe Vanilla Bean Pastry Cream (page 50), chilled thoroughly

FOR THE BUNS
⅓ cup whole milk
1 large egg, at room temperature
⅓ cup sour cream, at room temperature
1 teaspoon pure vanilla extract
2¼ cups plus 2 tablespoons all-purpose flour
2¼ teaspoons (1 package) active dry yeast
1 teaspoon kosher salt
½ cup sugar
5 tablespoons unsalted butter, softened
⅓ cup sliced blanched almonds, toasted, for garnish

FOR THE HONEY CARAMEL GLAZE
⅓ cup firmly packed light brown sugar
3 tablespoons heavy cream
3 tablespoons clover honey
2 tablespoons cold unsalted butter, cut into ½-inch pieces
¼ teaspoon fresh lemon juice

BEFORE YOU START

Line two cookie sheets with parchment paper or aluminum foil.

TO MAKE THE BUNS

1. In the bowl of an electric mixer fitted with the whip attachment, combine the milk, egg, sour cream, vanilla, and one-half of the flour. Mix on medium speed until it is a sticky paste.

2. Change the mixer attachment to the dough hook. Add the remaining flour, yeast, salt, and sugar, and mix on low speed to combine. Add the butter in pieces and beat on medium speed for 10 to 15 minutes until the dough forms a ball and is no longer sticking to the sides of the bowl. The dough should be nice and elastic.

3. Place the dough in a lightly greased bowl and cover it with plastic wrap. Set aside in a warm place to rise until doubled in volume, 2 to 3 hours.

4. When the dough has doubled in volume, punch it down and turn it out onto a work surface. Divide it into 12 even pieces, each weighing about 2 ounces.

5. Roll the dough into balls and place them about 2½ inches apart on the prepared cookie sheets (6 on each pan). Spray lightly with nonstick vegetable cooking spray and cover with plastic wrap (or lightly butter one side of the plastic wrap). Refrigerate overnight.

6. When you are ready for the final rise, remove the buns from the refrigerator. Bring about 3 quarts water to a boil. Place an empty roasting pan large enough to hold the water on the bottom of your cold oven. Pour the boiling water into the pan.

7. Remove the plastic from the buns. Position a rack in the top and bottom thirds of your oven. Place the cookie sheets on the racks in the oven (do not turn it on!) and shut the door. The steam of the water will help the buns in their final rise. The buns will just about double in size in about 40 minutes. (If your fridge is on a super-cold setting, your buns may take a little longer to rise. If they need more time, just boil some more water and refill the roasting pan.) When the buns have doubled in volume, remove them (and the roasting pan filled with water) from the oven.

8. Preheat the oven to 350°F.

9. Bake for 30 minutes, or until golden brown.

10. Remove to a wire rack to cool completely before filling.

TO MAKE THE GLAZE

1. In a small saucepan over medium heat, bring the brown sugar, heavy cream, honey, and butter to a boil. Cook for 30 seconds more, then remove the pan from the heat.

2. Stir in the lemon juice and let cool slightly.

TO COMPLETE THE BUNS

1. Poke a hole through the side of each bun, and hollow it out a bit. I find it easiest to do this with the pointy end of a stick thermometer or a metal skewer. Poke a hole large enough for an Ateco #801 ¼-inch round pastry tip to fit into. Once the stick is inside the bun, wiggle it from side to side, making room for the cream. Be careful not to poke through the other side—you don't want any of that cream coming out!

2. Whisk the pastry cream until smooth. Put it into the pastry bag fitted with the tip. Fill each bun with as much cream as you can without its spilling out. You should be able to fit at least 2 tablespoons into each bun.

3. Holding a bun upside down, dip the top of each bun into the honey caramel, and then sprinkle with the almonds. Repeat with the remaining buns. Bee Stings are best eaten as soon as they are made, but stay yummy all day.

PRO TIP: Freeze the buns! Once you form the dough into buns, you can place them in the freezer uncovered on the sheet before they start to rise again. Once they are frozen, cover with plastic wrap. They will keep frozen for up to 1 week. When you are ready to bake, take them from the freezer, and let them thaw unwrapped at room temperature. Proceed with the final rising before baking.

VANILLA BEAN PASTRY CREAM

Makes 1½ cups pastry cream

1 cup whole milk
¼ cup sugar
¼ vanilla bean, split, or ¾ teaspoon pure vanilla extract
3 large egg yolks
2 tablespoons cornstarch
2 tablespoons cold unsalted butter

1. Fill a medium saucepan with 3 inches of water and bring to a simmer. Set a bowl over the top, but make sure that the bottom of the bowl does not touch the water. (Remove the bowl and use it for the egg yolk mixture.)

2. In a separate saucepan, stir together the milk, half of the sugar, and the vanilla seeds and pod and heat to scalding, or until the milk is steaming and tiny bubbles are forming on the edges. Do not boil. If using vanilla extract, add it at the end of the recipe after the butter.

3. In the reserved bowl, whisk together the egg yolks and the remaining half of sugar until pale yellow. Whisk in the cornstarch. Little by little, whisk the hot milk into the egg mixture.

4. Place the bowl in the top of the double boiler, over simmering, not boiling, water. Cook, constantly whisking, until thick, about 5 minutes.

5. Remove from the heat and whisk in the butter and vanilla extract, if using. Lay a sheet of plastic wrap over the surface of the custard (to prevent a skin from forming) and refrigerate in an airtight container for up to 4 days. Whisk until smooth before using.

CHAPTER TWO

AFTER-SCHOOL SNACK

Cookies, Brownies, and Bars

Butterscotch Cashew Bars

Snickerdoodles

Chocolate Chip Cookies with Toasted Almonds

Double Dark Chocolate Cherry Cookies

Chestnut Honey Madeleines

Gingersnaps

Chewy Peanut Butter Cookies

Black Bottom Brownies

Honey Beescotti

Sour Cherry and Almond Biscotti

Chocolate Orange Macaroons

Pistachio Linzer Thumbprints

Toasted Almond Lemon Bars

Spiced Pumpkin Cookie Cakes

Chocolate Walnut Brownies

Pecan Shortbread Cookies

Strawberry Lemonade

AFTER-SCHOOL CHOCOLATE CHIPS

NOW YOU KNOW I love to eat chocolate chip cookies for break-fast, but I also love chocolate chip cookies after school. Well, not anymore, but years ago it was the highlight of my day. I remember smiling as I saw my dog, Brandy, racing toward the school bus to greet me after another harried day of third-grade activity. I'd jump off the bus, and we'd skip home (I skipped; I skipped everywhere in third grade), where my mom would have just baked a batch of my favorite cookies. (I am one of the lucky ones. My mom is a whiz in the kitchen, she sewed all of my dresses, she is an avid gardener, and she's beau-tiful, too!) She always made my after-school snack special, and she was always so happy to see me.

BUTTERSCOTCH CASHEW BARS

I love cashews, and they are not used nearly enough in baking. The combination of the shortbread crust, butterscotch caramel, and roasted cashews is stupendous. You can follow the cutting instructions I give, or cut them as small (or as large!) as you like.

Makes 2 dozen bars

½ pound (2 sticks) unsalted butter, softened
1 cup firmly packed light brown sugar
1¼ teaspoons kosher salt
2½ cups all-purpose flour
11 ounces butterscotch chips
¾ cup light corn syrup
1 tablespoon plus 1 teaspoon water
2 cups roasted salted whole cashews

BEFORE YOU START

Position a rack in the center of your oven. Preheat the oven to 350°F. Spray a 9 × 13-inch pan with nonstick vegetable cooking spray. Make a parchment "sling" by cutting two pieces of parchment paper, measuring 16½ inches long by 12 inches wide (you can also use aluminum foil). Place one piece across the length, and the other across the width of the pan, with the excess hanging over the edges. You will use this sling later to lift the finished bar from the pan. Spray the sling with the cooking spray.

1. In the bowl of an electric mixer fitted with the paddle attachment, cream together the butter, brown sugar, and salt on medium speed, 1 to 1½ minutes. Decrease the speed to low, add the flour, and mix until just combined.

2. Press the dough lightly and evenly onto the bottom of the prepared pan and poke holes all over with a fork. Bake for 35 to 40 minutes, or until the crust turns a golden color. Remove to a wire rack to cool.

3. Meanwhile, in a large heavy-bottomed saucepan over low heat, stir together the butterscotch chips, corn syrup, and water and heat, stirring until the mixture comes to a simmer and the chips are melted. Remove from the heat and pour the mixture evenly over the prebaked crust.

4. Sprinkle the cashews over the butterscotch caramel and return the pan to the oven for 5 minutes. Remove to a wire rack to cool completely.

5. Use a sharp knife to loosen the edges and, with the excess paper, lift the bars out of the pan. (If this proves difficult, pop the pan into a 300°F oven for a few minutes to warm the butterscotch slightly, and the bars will release more easily.)

CUT IT LIKE A PRO!

INVERT THE BARS onto a cutting board that is at least a little larger than the pan, and peel off the paper. Leave the bars upside down on the cutting board and, using a bread knife, gently score through the shortbread layer (not the caramel layer). You can score the long side in half and then each half into 3 even pieces, measuring a little more than 2 inches each. Do a quarter turn and score the short side in half, and then each half in half again, marking 24 squares, measuring roughly 2 inches by 2¼ inches. Using a chef's knife, cut through the butterscotch caramel layer where you have scored the bars with the bread knife.

The bars will keep in an airtight container at room temperature for up to 3 days. For longer storage, they can be wrapped in plastic wrap and refrigerated for up to 5 days, or frozen wrapped in plastic wrap and then aluminum foil for up to 3 weeks. Do not unwrap before defrosting.

SNICKERDOODLES

These are those yummy chewy old-fashioned cinnamon sugar cookies that everyone loves. They are the definition of "after-school snack."　　**Makes 3 dozen cookies**

FOR THE DOUGH
½ pound (2 sticks) unsalted butter, softened
1½ cups sugar
2 large eggs
2¾ cups all-purpose flour
1½ teaspoons cream of tartar
1 teaspoon baking soda
¼ teaspoon kosher salt

FOR THE CINNAMON SUGAR
1½ teaspoons ground cinnamon
½ cup sugar

1. In the bowl of an electric mixer fitted with the paddle attachment, cream the butter and sugar until smooth, 2 to 3 minutes. Add the eggs and mix until combined.

2. In a separate bowl, whisk together the flour, cream of tartar, baking soda, and salt. Add to the butter mixture and mix on low speed until combined. The dough will be soft and too sticky to roll. Refrigerate until firm, about 1 hour.

3. Position a rack in the top and bottom thirds of your oven. Preheat the oven to 350°F. Line two cookie sheets with parchment paper or aluminum foil.

4. *For the cinnamon sugar:* Combine the cinnamon and sugar in a small bowl.

5. Using a 1-ounce cookie scoop, or a tablespoon, shape the dough into balls and then roll them in the cinnamon sugar.

6. Place the cookies 2 inches apart on the prepared cookie sheets. Flatten them slightly with your fingertips so that they stay put. Bake for about 12 to 13 minutes, or until the bottoms are slightly golden in color. These cookies are supposed to be chewy, so do not overbake. Remove to a wire rack to cool.

Snickerdoodles keep in an airtight container at room temperature for up to 4 days. For longer storage, freeze well wrapped in plastic wrap and then aluminum foil for up to 3 weeks. Do not uncover before defrosting.

CHOCOLATE CHIP COOKIES WITH TOASTED ALMONDS

I would have to say that these are the all-time bestseller at Sweet Melissa's. I know, of all the things we bake day in and day out, chocolate chip cookies are the favorite? Just goes to show how true our philosophy is: to bake "everyone's favorite desserts, better than they've had them before."

Makes 24 cookies

½ cup whole natural almonds, toasted (see Note)
10 tablespoons unsalted butter, softened
½ cup granulated sugar
½ cup firmly packed light brown sugar
½ teaspoon pure vanilla extract
1 large egg
1⅔ cups all-purpose flour
¾ teaspoon baking soda
¼ teaspoon salt
8 ounces best-quality semisweet (58%) chocolate,
  coarsely chopped into ¼- to ½-inch chunks

BEFORE YOU START

Position a rack in the center of your oven. Preheat the oven to 350°F. Line two cookie sheets with parchment paper.

1. Roughly chop the almonds into large pieces.

2. In the bowl of an electric mixer fitted with the paddle attachment, cream together the butter, granulated sugar, brown sugar, and vanilla until fluffy, about 3 minutes. Add the egg and beat for another minute.

3. In a separate bowl, whisk together the flour, baking soda, and salt.

4. With the mixer on low speed, add the flour mixture in three batches, mixing until no flour is visible after each addition. Scrape down the sides of the bowl.

5. Remove the bowl from the mixer. Stir in the almonds and chocolate. Refrigerate the dough until firm, about 1 hour. (If you're really impatient or hungry, spread out the

dough on a tray or cookie sheet, lay a sheet of plastic wrap flush against the surface of the dough, and freeze so it chills up fast.)

6. Once the dough is chilled, turn it out onto a clean work surface and divide it in half. Roll each half into a log about 12 inches long. Refrigerate the logs for at least 30 minutes before slicing. (At this point, you can wrap the logs tightly in plastic wrap and then aluminum foil and freeze for up to 1 month.)

7. Cut the logs into 1-inch slices, and place them about 1½ inches apart on each cookie sheet. Bake for 13 to 14 minutes, or until the centers no longer have a glossy look of raw dough. They should be chewy, so do not overbake.

The cookies can be stored in an airtight container at room temperature for up to 3 days. For longer storage, refrigerate in an airtight container for up to 5 days, or freeze for up to 3 weeks. Do not uncover before defrosting.

TO TOAST NUTS

Preheat the oven to 350°F. Spread the almonds (or other nuts) in a single layer on a cookie sheet. Bake for 10 to 12 minutes, or until lightly golden and you can smell them. Remove to a wire rack to cool.

DOUBLE DARK CHOCOLATE CHERRY COOKIES

This cookie dough, even without the chocolate chips and sour cherries, is incredible. With the chocolate and the cherries? Totally overboard! I have seen the reaction to the first bite of this cookie so many times, and it's always the same. The eaters' eyes pop out a little and they look straight into my eyes while they continue to chew with their mouths closed. (I don't think they're being polite; I think they don't want to lose any!) When they finally swallow, they say, "Oh my God." Ooo—I love it.

Makes 2 dozen cookies

1 cup all-purpose flour
¾ cup best-quality unsweetened Dutch-process cocoa powder
1 teaspoon baking soda
¼ teaspoon kosher salt
8 tablespoons (1 stick) unsalted butter, softened 1½ sticks better
⅔ cup granulated sugar
¼ cup firmly packed dark brown sugar
1 large egg
¼ teaspoon pure vanilla extract
¾ cup best-quality semisweet (58%) chocolate chips
⅓ cup dried sour cherries

1. In a medium bowl, whisk together the flour, cocoa powder, baking soda, and salt.

2. In the bowl of an electric mixer fitted with the paddle attachment, cream together the butter, granulated sugar, and brown sugar until fluffy, about 3 minutes. Add the egg, mixing well. Stir in the vanilla.

3. With the mixer on low speed, add the flour mixture in three batches, mixing just until incorporated after each addition. Stir in the chocolate chips and cherries. Scrape down the sides of the bowl.

4. Refrigerate the dough for a few hours until firm. (If you're really impatient or hungry, spread the dough out on a tray or cookie sheet, lay a sheet of plastic wrap flush against the surface of the dough, and freeze so it chills up fast.)

5. Turn the dough out onto a clean work surface and divide it in half. Roll out into 2 uniform logs about 12 inches long. Refrigerate until firm enough to slice, about

1 hour. (At this point, you can wrap the logs tightly in plastic wrap and then aluminum foil and freeze for up to 1 month.)

6. Position a rack in the top and bottom thirds of your oven. Preheat the oven to 350°F. Line two cookie sheets with parchment paper or aluminum foil.

7. Cut the logs into 1-inch slices and place 1½ inches apart on the prepared cookie sheets. Bake for 15 minutes, or until the dough looks just baked. These cookies should be tender, so do not overbake.

The cookies can be stored in an airtight container at room temperature for up to 3 days. For longer storage, refrigerate in an airtight container for up to 5 days, or freeze for up to 3 weeks. Do not uncover before defrosting.

CHESTNUT HONEY MADELEINES

Melissa Clark, a very talented (and my favorite) food writer for The New York Times, *once wrote about my chestnut honey madeleines: "Delicate brown, dusted with sugar and scallop shaped, the chestnut honey madeleines at Sweet Melissa Pâtisserie in Brooklyn look just like ordinary madeleines. But one bite proves otherwise. A perfumed, almost autumnal sensation fills the mouth, like the scent of sunshine-dried leaves, butterscotch, and toasted nuts. Then the featherweight cake dissolves, leaving you to wonder: Could all that flavor really have come from such a dainty morsel? . . ."* (The New York Times, February 17, 1999)

No wonder she's my favorite food writer.   **Makes 2 dozen cookies**

⅔ **cup roasted hazelnuts**
1⅔ **cups confectioners' sugar, plus more for dusting**
½ **cup plus 1 tablespoon all-purpose flour**
13 **tablespoons unsalted butter**
6 **large egg whites**
1 **tablespoon chestnut or clover honey**

BEFORE YOU START

Using a pastry brush, brush on soft butter and then flour two 12-cup madeleine molds. Refrigerate until ready to use.

1. In the bowl of a food processor fitted with the metal blade, grind the hazelnuts with ⅔ cup of the confectioners' sugar, pulsing as fine as you can get it, so that it is a semicoarse flour (you should have ½ cup hazelnut flour).

2. In a large bowl, whisk together the hazelnut flour, all-purpose flour, and the remaining confectioners' sugar.

3. In a small heavy-bottomed saucepan over medium heat, melt the butter until the butter solids at the bottom of the pan turn golden brown. Immediately remove from the heat and strain into a bowl to stop the cooking. Discard the solids.

4. In the bowl of an electric mixer fitted with the whip attachment, beat the egg whites until foamy. Add the flour mixture and mix until combined. Add the butter and honey and mix until combined.

5. Spoon the batter into the prepared molds, filling almost to the top. Refrigerate for 2 hours.

6. Position a rack in the top and bottom thirds of your oven. Preheat the oven to 375°F.

7. Remove the filled molds from the refrigerator. Bake for 15 to 20 minutes, or until golden brown. After removing from the oven, immediately tap the pans on your work surface to release the madeleines. Transfer to a rack to cool completely.

To serve, turn the madeleines scallop side up and dust with confectioners' sugar. They will keep in an airtight container at room temperature for 3 days. For longer storage, refrigerate in an airtight container for up to 5 days, or freeze for up to 3 weeks. Do not uncover before defrosting.

GINGERSNAPS

Truth be told? We started giving out these gingersnaps to the babies who would come into the shop and start crying. It was a surefire way to make them happy! Now they come in and cry for *the gingersnaps. Needless to say, we give away a lot of gingersnaps. Adults love these simple spicy buttery cookies, too. Try them dipped in hot chocolate—crazy good. But you know who loves them the most? My horse, Mouse. They are how I trained her to nicker for me when I walk into the barn. Now I can't get her nose out of my pockets.*

Makes 4½ dozen cookies

½ cup granulated sugar
½ cup firmly packed light brown sugar
½ pound (2 sticks) unsalted butter, softened
1 large egg
⅓ cup molasses
2¼ cups all-purpose flour
½ teaspoon kosher salt
2 teaspoons baking soda
2 teaspoons ground ginger
1 teaspoon ground cinnamon
½ teaspoon ground allspice
¼ teaspoon freshly ground white pepper

1. In the bowl of an electric mixer fitted with the paddle attachment, cream the sugars and butter until light and fluffy, 1 to 1½ minutes. Beat in the egg. Stir in the molasses.

2. In a separate bowl, whisk together the flour, salt, baking soda, ginger, cinnamon, allspice, and white pepper.

3. Add the flour mixture to the butter mixture in three batches, mixing well after each addition. Scrape down the sides of the bowl. Refrigerate for at least 1 hour.

4. Position a rack in the center of your oven. Preheat the oven to 350°F. Line a cookie sheet with parchment paper or aluminum foil (see Pro tip).

5. Using a small cookie scoop, form balls approximately 1 inch in diameter, and place them 2 inches apart on the prepared cookie sheet. Bake for about 15 minutes. Remove to a wire rack to cool completely.

The cookies will keep in an airtight container at room temperature for up to 3 days. For longer storage, wrap in plastic wrap and refrigerate for up to 5 days, or freeze well wrapped in plastic wrap and then aluminum foil for up to 3 weeks. Do not unwrap before defrosting.

PRO TIP: You'll need three cookie sheets to bake all of the dough, but if you have only one sheet, between batches, cool it down quickly under cold water and reuse it—don't forget to dry it off!

Instantly recognizable for their crosshatch pattern, peanut butter cookies rank way up there among our favorite cookies. I feel like everyone must have had the pleasure of baking peanut butter cookies, or at least gingerly pressing the crosshatch pattern into the dough with a fork. However, just in case there are a few of you out there who haven't, here is the recipe. The cookies are best when they are chewy, so don't over-bake them!

Makes 2 dozen cookies

½ **cup smooth peanut butter**
8 **tablespoons (1 stick) unsalted butter**
½ **cup granulated sugar**
½ **cup firmly packed light brown sugar**
1 **large egg**
1¼ **cups all-purpose flour**
½ **teaspoon baking powder**
¾ **teaspoon baking soda**
¼ **teaspoon salt**

BEFORE YOU START

Position a rack in the top and bottom thirds of your oven. Preheat the oven to 325°F. Line two cookie sheets with parchment paper or aluminum foil.

1. In the bowl of an electric mixer fitted with the paddle attachment, cream the peanut butter with the butter and sugars until light and fluffy, 3 to 4 minutes. Beat in the egg.

2. In a separate bowl, whisk together the flour, baking powder, baking soda, and salt.

3. Add the flour mixture to the peanut butter mixture and mix until combined. Be sure to scrape down the sides of the bowl so that everything is combined evenly.

4. Scoop dough by the rounded tablespoonful and roll into balls. Place the balls about 2 inches apart on the prepared cookie sheets, and press down slightly. Using a fork dipped in flour, press down on the cookies first one way and then the other to form an "X" pattern, creating the crosshatch effect. (The cookies should now measure approximately 2 inches in diameter.) Bake for 10 minutes, or until the edges are

lightly golden. Overbaking will cause these chewy cookies to become crunchy, so try to avoid it.

The cookies will keep in an airtight container at room temperature for up to 3 days. For longer storage, they can be frozen wrapped in plastic wrap and aluminum foil for up to 1 month. Do not unwrap before defrosting.

This recipe is from my friend Stephanie Goldberg, chef and owner of Foodstyle, the catering company I worked for right out of culinary school. These are really great because they combine two of everyone's favorite desserts, brownies and cheesecake!

Makes 1 dozen big brownies

FOR THE BROWNIE BOTTOM
6 ounces best-quality unsweetened chocolate
½ pound (2 sticks) unsalted butter
1⅔ cups all-purpose flour
½ teaspoon baking powder
½ teaspoon kosher salt
4 large eggs plus 2 large egg yolks
2 cups sugar
1 tablespoon pure vanilla

FOR THE CHEESECAKE LAYER
1 pound (two 8-ounce packages) cream cheese, at room
  temperature
1½ cups sugar
¼ teaspoon kosher salt
6 large eggs
1½ teaspoons pure vanilla extract
2 cups (one 12-ounce package) semisweet (58%) chocolate
  chips

BEFORE YOU START

Position a rack in the center of your oven. Preheat the oven to 325°F. Lightly butter a 9 × 13-inch pan. Line the pan with parchment paper or aluminum foil.

TO MAKE THE BROWNIES

1. In the top of a double boiler over simmering, not boiling water, melt the chocolate and the butter, stirring to combine. Set aside to cool to warm.

2. In a medium bowl, whisk together the flour, baking powder, and salt.

3. In a large bowl, whisk together the eggs, egg yolks, sugar, and vanilla until smooth.

4. Pour the chocolate mixture into the egg mixture and combine with a whisk. Add the flour mixture to the chocolate/egg mixture and stir until just combined. Pour the brownie batter into the prepared pan, and spread evenly.

TO MAKE THE CHEESECAKE LAYER

In the bowl of an electric mixer fitted with the paddle attachment, cream together the cream cheese, sugar, and the salt until light and fluffy, about 5 minutes. Add the eggs, 2 at a time, and mix well after each addition. Scrape down the sides of the bowl. Stir in the vanilla.

TO COMPLETE THE BROWNIES

1. Pour the cheesecake mixture over the brownie layer. Sprinkle the chocolate chips evenly over the cheesecake layer.

2. Bake for about 1 hour and 15 minutes, or until lightly golden. Remove to a wire rack to cool. Cool completely before slicing and store in an airtight container in the refrigerator. May be served cold or at room temperature.

Store the brownies in a single layer in an airtight container in the refrigerator for up to 1 week. For longer storage, freeze in an airtight container for up to 2 weeks. Do not uncover before defrosting.

HONEY BEESCOTTI

I love these biscotti. The honey, candied orange peel, and caraway seeds make them so special, they really are the best thing to dunk into a hot cup of coffee. Candied orange peel can be found at most candy stores. Do try to find it; you won't believe what it does to these cookies.
Makes 3 dozen biscotti

4 tablespoons (½ stick) unsalted butter, softened
¾ cup sugar
3 tablespoons chestnut honey (or any flavor, including clover)
½ teaspoon kosher salt
2 large eggs
1½ teaspoons pure vanilla extract
1½ teaspoons almond extract
3 tablespoons coarsely chopped candied orange peel
1¾ cups all-purpose flour
1 teaspoon baking powder
2 teaspoons caraway seeds
½ cup whole natural almonds, coarsely chopped

BEFORE YOU START

Line a cookie sheet with parchment paper or aluminum foil.

1. In the bowl of an electric mixer fitted with the paddle attachment, cream the butter, sugar, honey, and salt until light and fluffy, 3 to 4 minutes. Add the eggs, vanilla, and almond extract and mix until combined. Add the candied orange peel and beat on high speed for 20 seconds.

2. In a separate bowl, whisk together the flour, baking powder, and caraway seeds.

3. Add the flour mixture to the butter mixture in three batches, mixing well after each addition. Scrape down the sides of the bowl. Stir in the almonds.

4. Turn the dough out onto the prepared cookie sheet, flatten, and refrigerate until firm, about 1 hour.

5. On a lightly floured board, divide the dough in half. Using a little extra flour if the dough feels sticky, roll each half into a log about 14 inches long. Refrigerate the logs until firm, about 30 minutes.

6. Position a rack in the center of your oven. Preheat the oven to 350°F. Line the cookie sheet with clean parchment paper.

7. Place the logs 4 inches apart on the prepared cookie sheet. Bake for about 30 minutes, or until the logs are lightly golden and slightly firm. Remove to a wire rack to cool. Turn down the oven to 275°F.

8. As soon as the logs are cool enough to handle but still warm, about 10 minutes, carefully peel them off the parchment paper and transfer to a cutting board. Using a serrated bread knife, gently score the logs at ¾-inch intervals on a 45-degree angle. After scoring, cut through each scored line in one motion with a sharp chef's knife, slicing the logs into pieces.

9. Carefully transfer the cookies to a freshly lined cookie sheet browned side down and not touching one another. Bake for an additional 25 minutes, rotate the pan, and continue to bake for another 20 minutes. Remove to a wire rack to cool on the pan to room temperature.

The biscotti will keep in an airtight container at room temperature for at least 1 week. For longer storage, tightly wrap in plastic wrap and then aluminum foil and freeze for up to 3 weeks. Do not unwrap before defrosting.

SOUR CHERRY AND ALMOND BISCOTTI

My sister-in-law Randi loves this cookie. I bring them to her every Christmas. Every year she says they are her best present. **Makes 3 dozen biscotti**

½ cup dried sour cherries
½ cup fresh orange juice
4 tablespoons (½ stick) unsalted butter, at room temperature
1 cup sugar
Zest of 1 lemon
¼ teaspoon salt
2 large eggs
1½ teaspoons pure vanilla extract
1½ teaspoons almond extract
1¾ cups all-purpose flour
1 teaspoon baking powder
½ cup whole blanched almonds, roughly chopped

BEFORE YOU START

Line a cookie sheet with parchment paper or aluminum foil.

1. In a small saucepan over low heat, combine the cherries and orange juice and bring to a simmer. Remove from the heat, cover, and let the cherries reconstitute.

2. In the bowl of an electric mixer fitted with the paddle attachment, cream the butter, sugar, zest, and salt until light and fluffy, 3 to 4 minutes. Add the eggs, one at a time, mixing well after each addition. Scrape down the sides of the bowl. Add the vanilla and almond extract.

3. In a separate bowl, whisk together the flour and baking powder.

4. Add the flour mixture to the butter mixture in three batches, mixing well after each addition. Scrape down the sides of the bowl.

5. Drain the cherries, discarding the juice. Stir the cherries and almonds into the dough.

6. Turn the dough out onto the prepared cookie sheet, flatten, and refrigerate until firm, about 1 hour.

7. On a lightly floured work surface, divide the dough in half. Using a little extra flour if the dough is sticky, roll each half into a log about 14 inches long.

8. Position a rack in the center of your oven. Preheat the oven to 350°F. Line the cookie sheet with clean parchment paper.

9. Place the logs about 4 inches apart on the prepared cookie sheet. Bake for 30 minutes, or until the logs are lightly golden and slightly firm. Remove to a wire rack to cool. Turn down the oven to 275°F.

10. As soon as the logs are cool enough to handle but still warm, about 10 minutes, carefully peel them off the paper and transfer to a cutting board. Using a serrated bread knife, gently score the logs at ¾-inch intervals on a 45-degree angle. After scoring, cut through each scored line in one motion with a sharp chef's knife, slicing the logs into pieces.

11. Carefully transfer the cookies to a freshly lined cookie sheet browned side down and not touching one another. Bake for an additional 60 minutes, rotating the cookie sheet after 30 minutes. Remove to a wire rack to cool on the pan to room temperature.

The biscotti will keep in an airtight container at room temperature for at least 1 week. For longer storage, tightly wrap in plastic wrap and then aluminum foil and freeze for up to 3 weeks. Do not unwrap before defrosting.

CHOCOLATE ORANGE MACAROONS

When I tell people I own Sweet Melissa's, they often say "Oh! I love your macaroons!"
You want an easy recipe? These are easy. Really easy. **Makes 2 dozen cookies**

6 ounces best-quality solid semisweet (58%) chocolate
One 14-ounce bag sweetened coconut
Zest of 1 orange
1 cup sugar
3 large egg whites

BEFORE YOU START

Position a rack in the center of your oven. Preheat the oven to 325°F. Line a cookie sheet with parchment paper or aluminun foil.

1. Using a serrated bread knife, finely chop the chocolate. Set aside.

2. In a large bowl, combine the coconut and zest, and rub together with your hands. (This will break up the coconut and release the orange oils.)

3. Stir in the sugar and chocolate to the coconut and mix to combine. Add the egg whites. Use your hands to mix until everything is coated and the egg whites are distributed evenly.

4. Using a 1-ounce cookie scoop, firmly pack the dough into the scoop and unmold about 2 inches apart onto the prepared cookie sheet. Bake for 25 to 30 minutes, or until the cookies are golden brown. Remove to a wire rack to cool completely.

The cookies keep in an airtight container at room temperature for up to 3 days. For longer storage, wrap in plastic wrap and refrigerate for up to 5 days, or freeze well wrapped in plastic wrap and then aluminum foil for up to 3 weeks. Do not unwrap before defrosting.

PRO TIP: If you want to, make the cookie base up to 1 week ahead! Just keep it in an airtight container in the refrigerator and bake the cookies when you have time. (These just keep getting easier.)

Lemon Coconut Macaroons

Omit the chocolate and the orange zest. Add the zest and juice of 1 lemon to the co-conut and use only 2 egg whites. The recipe makes slightly fewer cookies, about 20 altogether.

PISTACHIO LINZER THUMBPRINTS

These delicious cookies are fun to make; I love that I have to poke my fingers in them to make room for the jam filling. Doing that reminds me of when I used to bake with my little sister, Erin. She wanted to be in charge of poking the holes. I'd have to go back over them when she wasn't looking because her tiny fingers made holes too small for the filling!

Makes about 4 dozen cookies

1 cup shelled unsalted pistachios, plus ⅔ cup shelled unsalted pistachios, finely chopped, for rolling
2¼ cups all-purpose flour
⅔ cup sugar
1 teaspoon baking powder
1 teaspoon ground cinnamon
¼ teaspoon kosher salt
½ pound (2 sticks) very cold, unsalted butter, cut into ½-inch pieces
1 tablespoon freshly grated lemon zest
2 large eggs, separated
1 teaspoon pure vanilla extract
½ cup seedless raspberry or apricot preserves
Confectioners' sugar, for sprinkling

1. In a food processor fitted with a metal blade, pulse the 1 cup of pistachios with ½ cup of the flour until fine but not powdery. Add the remaining 1¾ cups flour, the sugar, baking powder, cinnamon, and salt. Pulse to combine.

2. Carefully add the butter cubes and zest and toss with your fingers to coat with flour. Pulse until the mixture looks like cornmeal. Add the egg yolks and vanilla and pulse until the dough just holds together.

3. Refrigerate the dough until firm, about 1 hour. (At this point, the dough can be wrapped tightly in plastic wrap and then aluminum foil and frozen for up to 3 weeks.)

4. Position a rack in the center of your oven. Preheat the oven to 350°F. Line two cookie sheets with parchment paper or aluminum foil.

5. Using a 1-ounce cookie scoop or a tablespoon, scoop the dough into 1-inch balls. Roll each ball in the egg whites and then in the chopped pistachios. Place the cookies 1½ inches apart on the prepared cookie sheets, and press down lightly with your fingers so that they stay put. Using a floured thumb (or your finger of choice), press an indentation into the center of each cookie.

6. Keep the cookies chilled while you fill a pastry bag fitted with a ¼-inch round pastry tip (I use an Ateco #801) with the preserves. (Alternatively, put the preserves in a resealable plastic bag, squeeze it down to the bottom, and snip off a little bit of one corner—instant piping bag!) Fill each cookie with about ¼ to ½ teaspoon preserves.

7. Bake for 20 minutes, or until lightly browned. Remove to a wire rack to cool.

8. When cool, generously dust with confectioners' sugar. Using your finger dipped in water, tap on the centers of each cookie, so that the jam shines through the sugar.

The cookies keep in an airtight container at room temperature for up to 3 days. For longer storage, wrap in plastic wrap and refrigerate for up to 5 days, or freeze well wrapped in plastic wrap and then aluminum foil for up to 3 weeks. Do not unwrap before defrosting. Dust with confectioners' sugar before serving.

SWITCH IT UP: Use hazelnuts instead of the pistachios and fill the thumbprint with seedless raspberry preserves. Done this way, these cookies will remind you of traditional linzer tarts.

TOASTED ALMOND LEMON BARS

Everyone loves lemon bars. I make mine extra special by adding toasted almonds to the shortbread crust.

Makes 1 dozen bars

FOR THE CRUST
2 cups all-purpose flour
¾ cup confectioners' sugar
½ cup sliced blanched almonds, lightly toasted (see page 59)
½ teaspoon salt
20 tablespoons (2½ sticks) cold, unsalted butter, cut into ¼-inch pieces

FOR THE LEMON FILLING
4 large eggs
1¾ cups sugar
½ teaspoon almond extract
½ cup all-purpose flour
¾ cup fresh lemon juice (about 7 lemons)
¼ cup confectioners' sugar for sprinkling

BEFORE YOU START

Position a rack in the center of your oven. Preheat the oven to 350°F. Spray a 9 × 13-inch pan with nonstick vegetable cooking spray. Make a parchment "sling" by cutting two pieces of parchment paper, measuring 16½ inches long by 12 inches wide (you can also use aluminum foil). Place one piece across the length, and the other across the width of the pan, with the excess hanging over the edges. You will use this sling later to lift the finished bar from the pan. Spray the sling with the cooking spray.

TO MAKE THE CRUST

1. In the bowl of a food processor fitted with the metal blade, pulse the flour, sugar, almonds, and salt to combine. Add the cold butter in pieces and pulse until the dough comes together in a ball.

2. Turn the dough out into the prepared pan and press evenly into the bottom and 1¼ inches up the sides. (This crust, once it is baked, needs to act as a liner in which to pour the liquidy lemon filling. So be sure to do a good job of pressing the dough up the sides—no cracks!) Cover the dough with a piece of parchment paper or aluminum foil, and fill with pie weights (you can use dried beans or uncooked rice as pie weights as well). Bake for 25 to 30 minutes, or until lightly golden. Carefully remove the pie weights and the liner and bake for an additional 10 to 15 minutes, or until the whole crust is golden. Remove to a wire rack to cool.

TO MAKE THE FILLING

In a medium bowl, whisk together the eggs and sugar until smooth. Add the almond extract and flour, and whisk until smooth. Add the lemon juice, and whisk to combine.

TO COMPLETE THE BARS

1. Pour the lemon filling into the prepared crust. Reduce the oven temperature to 325°F. Bake for 30 minutes, or until the filling is firm and lightly golden. Remove to a wire rack to cool.

2. When cool use the parchment sling to lift the entire bar from the pan and onto a cutting board. Slice into twelve 3 × 3½-inch bars. Remove from the pan and, using a small sifter, dust with the confectioners' sugar.

The bars keep in an airtight container at room temperature for up to 2 days. For longer storage, wrap in plastic wrap and refrigerate for up to 5 days, or freeze well wrapped in plastic wrap and then aluminum foil for up to 3 weeks. Do not unwrap before defrosting. Dust with confectioners' sugar before serving.

SPICED PUMPKIN COOKIE CAKES

You have to be very careful with these cookies. You can't give them to just anyone. If you make them for someone you are sweet on, he or she will fall instantly in love. If you are at odds with your lover, make these cookies. They will settle all disputes and improve communication almost immediately (well, as soon as they're eaten). They are really more like little cream cheese-filled pumpkin cakes than cookies, which is the reason they are so amazing, and why they fly out of the store. Get ready for some serious admirers.

Makes about 2 dozen cookie cakes

FOR THE COOKIE CAKES
½ **cup firmly packed light brown sugar**
½ **cup granulated sugar**
8 tablespoons (1 stick) unsalted butter, at room temperature
¼ **cup molasses**
1 large egg
1 cup pumpkin puree, fresh (see Note, page 197) or canned
2 cups all-purpose flour
1 teaspoon baking soda
1½ teaspoons ground cinnamon
½ **teaspoon freshly ground nutmeg**
¾ **teaspoon kosher salt**
½ **cup whole milk**
Confectioners' sugar, for dusting

FOR THE CREAM CHEESE FILLING
6 tablespoons unsalted butter, softened
6 tablespoons cream cheese, softened
¾ **cup confectioners' sugar**
¾ **teaspoon freshly grated orange zest (about ½ orange)**
½ **teaspoon pure vanilla extract**

BEFORE YOU START

Position a rack in the center of your oven. Preheat the oven to 350°F. Line a cookie sheet with parchment paper or aluminum foil.

TO MAKE THE COOKIE CAKES

1. In the bowl of an electric mixer fitted with the paddle attachment, mix together the brown and white sugars on low speed to get rid of any lumps. Add the butter, and beat together until light and fluffy, 1 to 1½ minutes. Add the molasses and egg, and mix to combine. Scrape down the sides of the bowl. Add the pumpkin puree and mix to combine.

2. In a separate bowl, whisk together the flour, baking soda, cinnamon, nutmeg, and salt.

3. Add the flour mixture to the pumpkin mixture in three batches, alternating with the milk. Mix well after each addition. Scrape down the sides of the bowl. Blend thoroughly, but do not overbeat.

4. Using a pastry bag fitted with an Ateco #808 ½-inch round pastry tip, pipe the dough into cookie cakes about 1½ inches in diameter onto the prepared cookie sheet. (Alternatively, drop the dough by rounded teaspoonfuls onto the prepared cookie sheet). Bake for 12 to 15 minutes, or until a wooden skewer inserted into the center of one of the cookies comes out clean. Remove to a wire rack to cool completely before filling.

TO MAKE THE FILLING

In the bowl of an electric mixer fitted with the paddle attachment, combine the butter, cream cheese, confectioners' sugar, zest, and vanilla. Start mixing on low speed and then continue on medium speed until just fluffy and smooth, 2 to 3 minutes. Do not overbeat.

TO COMPLETE THE COOKIE CAKES

1. Turn half of the cookie cakes upside down onto a freshly lined cookie sheet.

2. Using a pastry bag fitted with a ¼-inch round pastry tip (I use an Ateco #801) (or use a resealable plastic bag with a corner cut off or a teaspoon), pipe or place about 1 teaspoon of filling onto each upside-down cookie cake. Place the remaining cookie cake halves (right side up!) on top.

3. Refrigerate briefly until set, 15 to 20 minutes. Dust with confectioners' sugar before serving.

Keep the cookie cakes refrigerated in an airtight container for up to 4 days.

CHOCOLATE WALNUT BROWNIES

As you can imagine, I've tried a lot of brownie recipes. This one is based on Julia Child's recipe, so I had to try it. It is the best brownie I've ever met.

Makes 1 dozen brownies

- ½ pound (2 sticks) unsalted butter
  4 ounces best-quality unsweetened chocolate,
   coarsely chopped
  2 large eggs
  1½ cups sugar
  1 teaspoon pure vanilla extract
  1 cup all-purpose flour
  ½ teaspoon kosher salt
  ⅔ cup walnuts, coarsely chopped (optional)

BEFORE YOU START

Position a rack in the center of your oven. Preheat the oven to 350°F. Butter and flour a 9 × 9 × 2-inch square cake pan.

1. In the top of a double boiler set over simmering, not boiling, water, melt the butter and chocolate. Remove from the heat but keep warm.

2. In the bowl of an electric mixer fitted with the whip attachment, beat together the eggs, sugar, and vanilla on medium speed until pale yellow in color, about 2 minutes. Add the melted chocolate and mix to combine.

3. In a separate bowl, whisk together the flour and salt.

4. Add the flour mixture to the chocolate mixture in 3 batches, mixing on low speed until just combined. Do not overmix. Scrape down the sides of the bowl. Stir in the nuts by hand.

5. Pour the batter into the prepared pan. Bake for 45 to 50 minutes, or until sides begin to pull away from the pan and center is moist but not runny, and a wooden skewer inserted into the center comes out clean. Remove to a wire rack to cool.

6. When cool, loosen the edges of the pan with a knife and invert the brownies onto a cutting board. Cut into 12 brownies, measuring 3 inches by 2¼ inches, or serve straight from the pan.

The brownies keep in an airtight container at room temperature for up to 3 days. For longer storage, wrap in plastic wrap and refrigerate for up to 5 days, or freeze well wrapped in plastic wrap and then aluminum foil for up to 3 weeks. Do not unwrap before defrosting.

PECAN SHORTBREAD COOKIES

These cookies are similar to Mexican wedding cakes, and they are irresistible. The buttery toastiness of the pecans make them melt in your mouth. They are very small so you can eat a ton of them, and not feel guilty about it. They are too good for guilt.

Makes about 3 dozen cookies

10 tablespoons cold, unsalted butter, cut into pieces
¼ cup sugar
¼ teaspoon salt
1 teaspoon pure vanilla extract
1 cup all-purpose flour
1¼ cups shelled pecan pieces, finely chopped
2 cups confectioners' sugar, for coating

BEFORE YOU START

Position a rack in the center of your oven. Preheat the oven to 325°F. Line two cookie sheets with parchment paper or aluminum foil.

1. In the bowl of a food processor fitted with the metal blade, pulse the butter, sugar, and salt to combine. Add the vanilla, and pulse to combine. Add the flour and pecans, and pulse to combine. Remove the dough from the mixer.

2. Using a small cookie scoop or a tablespoon, form balls and place 1½ inches apart on the prepared cookie sheets. Bake for 25 to 30 minutes, or until the bottoms of the cookies are lightly golden. Remove to a wire rack to cool.

3. Put the confectioners' sugar in a medium bowl. When the cookies are almost cool, roll them in the sugar.

The cookies keep in an airtight container at room temperature for up to 3 days. For longer storage, wrap in plastic wrap and refrigerate for up to 5 days, or freeze well wrapped in plastic wrap and then aluminum foil for up to 3 weeks. Do not unwrap before defrosting. Roll in confectioners' sugar before serving.

STRAWBERRY LEMONADE

Huckleberry's restaurant was the closest I had come to heaven by age nine. It was, as I remember, a "fancy" restaurant, and expensive I'm sure, because we went only once a year—for lunch for my great grandma Alice's birthday. The reason I loved it so much? It wasn't just the food, although I remember it was delicious. It wasn't just the atmosphere, although I remember tall ceilings and big windows with sweeping views. My favorite part of Huckleberry's was the strawberry lemonade. They crushed strawberries to a pulp and stirred them into sweet tart lemonade. Sucking the drink through a straw was not always easy because of the bits of berry that would inevitably get caught. So I had to drink from the rim of the glass, which was a perfect solution, because the glass was rimmed with lemon juice and dipped in confectioners' sugar. It was meant for licking, and garnished with a whole berry. Yum.

Makes about 1½ quarts lemonade

¾ **cup sugar**
1 **cup very hot water**
1 **cup fresh lemon juice**
4½ **cups cold water**
1 **recipe Fresh Strawberry Sauce (page 210)**
Confectioners' sugar, for the glasses
Fresh strawberries for garnish

1. In a pitcher, combine the sugar and hot water and stir until the sugar has dissolved into a syrup. Stir in the lemon juice and cold water.

2. Add the strawberry sauce and stir to combine.

3. Pour over ice into tall glasses rimmed with confectioners' sugar. Garnish with fresh strawberries, if using.

Strawberry lemonade keeps at least 3 days in the refrigerator.

CHAPTER THREE

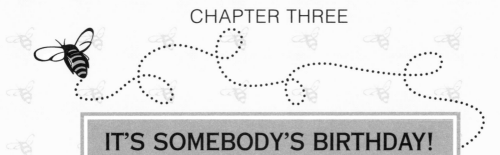

IT'S SOMEBODY'S BIRTHDAY!

Special Layer Cakes

I'VE ALWAYS LOVED the expression "It's the icing on the cake"—it means that there is something that is already wonderful and complete, and then you make it even better! But one thing is for sure: You have to start with a great cake. This is essential and, to me, the best part.

I was excited to write this chapter because I truly feel that each cake I've included is the best of its kind. These cakes are a result of years of perfecting. And these are recipes to use—you can multiply them if need be to fit larger pans, and you don't need to compute any special formulas to figure out how to adjust the leavener. They work as they are and you can bake them all with confidence.

These cakes are also the foundation of "Sweet Melissa's Wedding and Specialty Cakes" division, so for those of you who like to bake wedding cakes, this chapter will be an enormous help.

The vanilla butter cake, used in the Fluffy Coconut Cake recipe (page 96), should become your standard vanilla cake. I don't bother making any other. The only challenge with this cake is refraining from eating the batter—yes, even before it's baked, it's amazing.

The devil's food cake, which is my standard chocolate cake, is used in a few of the following recipes. It is so moist and delicious because I use the darkest Dutch-process cocoa powder, sour cream, and rich French roast hot coffee in the batter. It is so good and, as with all of these cakes, you'll want to eat it straight from the pan.

The cakes using freshly ground nut flours are extraspecial. The nut flours add a richness, a flavor, and a texture that are unmatched. I brown the butter in these batters, which adds depth, and the cake batters are lightened with meringue.

My carrot and red velvet cakes are classics. There are so many recipes for these two available, but after a lot of testing, I believe these to be the best. Both are amazing when finished with traditional cream cheese frosting. They are serious crowd pleasers.

The frostings and fillings in this chapter show a few of the many ways you can dress up these cakes even more. Once you get to know the flavors, you can have fun mixing and matching on your own. (Hint:

Passion fruit curd is delicious with sweet almond cake and fresh rasp-berries, no frosting needed.)

The cakes in this chapter are so uniquely delicious, yet the ingre-dients are so familiar. If you make any one of the cakes from this chapter, you will become somebody's hero!

HOW TO ASSEMBLE A LAYER CAKE

Assembling a layer cake seems as though it would be pretty straight forward, but there are a few tips that I use so that my results look con-sistent and professional.

First, the filling: Before you assemble your cake, be sure that your fillings are at the appropriate temperature. Fruit curds should be cold. Ganache fillings, buttercreams, and frostings should be at room tem-perature. Preserves can be cold or at room temperature.

Next, the cake: The layer cake recipes in this book are made up of two separate layers. Before you do anything, use a serrated knife to trim off any excess cake that has domed or risen up, and make your layers as flat and even as possible. Give the scraps to your kids or save them for something like trifle.

FOR UNSPLIT LAYER CAKES

If you are assembling an unsplit layer cake, as opposed to a split layer cake (page 93), once you have trimmed the layers as needed, you are ready to fill and frost them. Unsplit layer cakes tend to have sturdier fillings, so all they need is one nice thick layer between them.

To begin, cut 4 strips of wax or parchment paper about 12 inches long by 3 inches wide. Place the bottom cake layer trimmed side up on your serving plate. Tuck the wax paper under the edges of your cake on all sides. Later, after frosting the cake, you can pull away the strips to reveal a nice clean serving plate.

Using a metal offset spatula, spread the filling across the top of the layer, but leave about ½ inch uncovered around the outside edges. (This leaves room for the filling to be squished down but to stay inside the cake.)

Place the second layer trimmed side down on top of the filling and press down gently with your hands.

Now you can proceed to How to Crumb Coat and Frost a Layer Cake (see page 94).

FOR SPLIT LAYER CAKES

For fillings that are looser in texture, such as lemon curd, or fillings that taste best in smaller amounts, such as raspberry preserves, you will want *more* layers holding *less* filling. Therefore, you will need to split each trimmed cake layer in half. This can be done with a long serrated bread knife. If you're good, you can cut the layer without measuring and do so evenly. If you're not sure how good you are, you can use a ruler to measure and toothpicks to mark the center of the sides of the layer every 3 inches or so all around. Once you've marked the center all around, lay your knife above the toothpicks and cut through the layer as you turn the cake, always staying on top of the toothpicks and cutting until you have cut the layer completely in half. Don't separate the halves yet. Repeat with your second layer.

While the cake halves are still together, take a finger full of frosting and mark a vertical smear down the side of the cake, anywhere, from top to bottom, so that later you can line up the layers where they belong.

Slide each of the top layers onto a separate flat plate, or paper plate, and set aside.

Cut four strips of wax or parchment paper about 12 inches long by 3 inches wide. Place the bottom half of a cake layer cut side up on your serving plate. Tuck the wax paper under the edges of your cake on all sides. Later, after frosting the cake, you can pull away the strips to reveal a nice clean serving plate.

Using a metal offset spatula, spread the filling across the top of the layer but leave about ½ inch uncovered around the outside edges. (This leaves room for the filling to be squished down but to stay inside the cake.)

Place the matching half of the bottom layer over it cut side down. Spread filling over the trimmed top, leaving a ½ inch around the edges uncovered. (You know—squish room.)

Now place the reserved top half of the second layer trimmed side down on the second layer of filling. Spread it with filling, again leaving ½ inch around the edges uncovered.

Place the matching half of the second cake cut side down on top of the third layer of filling.

Using your hands, press gently on the center of the top layer to join the layers together. If you have the time, refrigerate the filled layer cake for at least 1 hour. Chilling will make the cake easier to frost.

HOW TO CRUMB COAT AND FROST A LAYER CAKE

You are going to frost your layer cake in two steps. The first step will be a crumb coat, which will keep most of the unsightly crumbs from ruining your finished frosting. To do this, simply apply a light, even layer of frosting on all sides of the cake. (*Really,* it doesn't matter what it looks like; it will be underneath the final frosting.) Place the cake in the refrigerator to chill for a good 30 minutes.

After the crumb coat has chilled, smooth on your final layer of frosting. It does take a lot of time to get it really smooth and perfect, so I prefer to make the frosting all swirly and peaked—it looks way more delicious this way as well.

If you must travel with your cake, finish it the night before, and refrigerate it overnight. Your layer cake will be a lot happier on the trip, and have the best odds of getting to the party in one piece.

FLUFFY COCONUT CAKE
WITH PASSION FRUIT FILLING

This is one of the most incredible layer cakes; the passion fruit curd in the center is such a delicious surprise! Your guests may not know what it is, but they will love it! Passion fruit juice is becoming more widely available in major cities, especially in specialty food stores and in the ethnic section of the supermarket. Instead of the passion fruit juice you can substitute lemon juice (just use ¾ cup fresh lemon juice as is, without reducing), and create another great classic combination—lemon and coconut! Yummy.

There are three components to this cake, as there are in most of my split layer cakes: the filling, the cake, and the frosting. If you have some time, you can spread out making these elements over a few days and make the whole process seem almost effortless.

Note: The fluffy white cake in this recipe is a phenomenal white cake. It is astonishing how delicious and moist it is; the texture is sublime! The trick to this cake is to efficiently incorporate the ingredients as thoroughly and quickly as possible, scrape down the sides of the bowl, and to not overbeat the batter before you fold in the meringue. Your careful attention to these details will be well rewarded.

Makes one 9-inch cake

FOR THE CAKE
20 tablespoons (2½) sticks unsalted butter, softened
2½ cups sugar
4¾ cups sifted cake flour
2¼ teaspoons baking powder
½ teaspoon kosher salt
1¾ cups whole milk
1 tablespoon plus 1½ teaspoons pure vanilla extract
9 large egg whites, at room temperature

FOR THE PASSION FRUIT FILLING
1½ cups passion fruit juice
1 tablespoon fresh lemon juice
7 large egg yolks
2 large eggs
¾ cup sugar

FOR THE COCONUT CREAM CHEESE FROSTING
8 ounces (1 package) cream cheese, softened
2 cups confectioners' sugar, sifted
½ pound (2 sticks) unsalted butter, softened
1 teaspoon pure vanilla extract
½ cup sweetened cream of coconut
3 cups sweetened coconut flakes

BEFORE YOU START

Place a rack in the center of your oven. Preheat the oven to 350°F. Butter and flour two 9 × 2-inch round cake pans. Line each with a 9-inch round of parchment paper.

TO MAKE THE CAKE

1. In the bowl of an electric mixer fitted with the paddle attachment, cream the butter and sugar on medium speed until light and fluffy, 2 to 3 minutes.

2. In separate large bowl, whisk together the cake flour, baking powder, and salt.

3. In a separate bowl, combine the milk and vanilla.

4. Add the flour mixture to the butter mixture in three batches, alternating with the milk, starting and ending with the flour mixture. Mix well after each addition but be careful not to overmix. Scrape down the sides of the bowl. Mix on medium-high speed for 10 seconds. Transfer the mixture to a large bowl.

5. In the very clean bowl of an electric mixer fitted with the very clean whip attachment, beat the egg whites on medium-high speed until they hold medium stiff peaks.

6. Using a rubber spatula, briskly fold one-third of the meringue mixture into the batter to lighten it. Gently fold in the remaining meringue until just combined.

7. Divide the batter equally between the two prepared cake pans. Use a spatula to level the batter. Bake for 40 to 45 minutes, or until the cake springs back when touched with your finger, and a wooden skewer inserted into the center comes out clean. Remove to a rack to cool for 30 minutes before turning out onto the rack to cool completely.

The baked layers may be stored tightly wrapped in plastic wrap at room temperature for 2 days. For longer storage, wrap tightly in plastic wrap and refrigerate for up to 4 days, or freeze wrapped in plastic wrap and then aluminum foil for up to 2 weeks. Do not unwrap before thawing.

TO MAKE THE FRUIT FILLING

1. In a medium skillet, bring the passion fruit juice to a boil. Turn down the heat to simmer, and reduce the fruit juice by half, about 10 minutes. (You will have ¾ cup passion fruit concentrate.) Allow to cool. Stir in the lemon juice.

2. In a medium bowl, whisk together the egg yolks, eggs, and sugar until well combined. Whisk the passion fruit concentrate into the egg mixture.

3. Set the bowl over a pot of simmering, not boiling, water. Be sure it is not touching the water. Cook, stirring, until *nappante* (thick enough to coat the back of a spoon) or 185°F on a candy thermometer, 5 to 7 minutes. Remove from the heat.

4. Strain the mixture into a bowl set in an ice bath (see Note).

5. Lay a sheet of plastic wrap flush against the surface of the filling (to prevent a skin from forming). Refrigerate until cold before using.

The fruit filling keeps in an airtight container in the refrigerator for up to 1 week.

TO MAKE THE FROSTING

1. In the bowl of an electric mixer fitted with the paddle attachment, cream together the cream cheese and confectioners' sugar on low speed, about 1 minute. Increase the speed to medium high and beat until fluffy and smooth, 2 minutes. Scrape down the sides of the bowl.

2. Add the butter and mix on medium speed until just combined, stopping once to scrape down the sides of the bowl, 1 to 2 minutes. Do not overbeat. Decrease the speed to low and add the vanilla and cream of coconut and mix until just combined.

Use immediately or store in an airtight container in the refrigerator for up to 3 days. Let the frosting come to room temperature and beat in the mixer slightly before using.

TO COMPLETE THE CAKE

1. See How to Assemble a Layer Cake (page 91) for instructions on how to fill and frost a split layer cake.

2. After the cake is frosted, use your hands to help pat the coconut onto the sides and the top of the cake.

Once completed, the layer cake may be stored in a cake saver in the refrigerator for up to 4 days.

Note: An ice bath is a large bowl filled with two quarts of ice and two cups of water. A smaller bowl containing a hot liquid is set inside the bath in order to help cool down the liquid quickly. Add more ice as needed.

PRO TIP: When you mix the ingredients for the frosting, start on the mixer's lowest speed and quickly turn on and off a few times so the confectioners' sugar doesn't fly everywhere. When the ingredients come together, increase the speed to medium high.

DEVIL'S FOOD CAKE
WITH PEANUT BUTTER FROSTING

Having been born on Thanksgiving meant that much of the time school was on break on my birthday. When my birthday did fall on a day when school was in session, I would be so excited at the chance to bring birthday cake in to the class, and to have the teacher lead us in a "Happy Birthday" to me!

Devil's Food Cake with Peanut Butter Frosting will make any child the envy of his or her classmates. Adults, too, love the moist chocolate cake and fluffy frosting that is reminiscent of birthdays past.

Makes one 9-inch cake

FOR THE CAKE

6 ounces best-quality unsweetened chocolate, coarsely chopped

⅔ cup vegetable or canola oil

2⅔ cups sugar

1⅔ cups all-purpose flour

⅓ cup best-quality unsweetened Dutch-process cocoa powder

1 teaspoon baking soda

¾ teaspoon kosher salt

⅔ cup sour cream

3 large eggs

1⅓ cups hot strong brewed coffee

FOR THE PEANUT BUTTER FROSTING

1 pound confectioners' sugar, sifted

1½ pounds unsalted butter, softened

2 teaspoons pure vanilla extract

3 tablespoons whole milk

½ cup smooth peanut butter, at room temperature

BEFORE YOU START

Position a rack in the center of your oven. Preheat the oven to 350°F. Butter and flour two 9 × 2-inch round cake pans. Line each pan with a 9-inch round of parchment paper.

TO MAKE THE CAKE

1. In the top of a double boiler set over simmering, not boiling, water, melt the chocolate, stirring occasionally. When the chocolate is completely melted, whisk in the vegetable oil until smooth. Remove from the heat, but keep warm over the hot water.

2. In the bowl of an electric mixer fitted with the paddle attachment, combine the sugar, flour, cocoa powder, baking soda, and salt, and mix well.

3. In a separate bowl, whisk together the sour cream and eggs until smooth.

4. Add the egg mixture to the flour mixture, and mix until combined. Be sure to scrape down the sides of the bowl. Add the melted chocolate mixture and mix until combined. Add the hot coffee in a stream, and mix until combined. (Again, scrape down the sides and bottom of the bowl.) The batter will be loose.

5. Divide the batter evenly between the prepared cake pans. Bake for 35 to 40 minutes, or until a wooden skewer inserted into the center comes out clean. Remove to a wire rack to cool in the pans for 25 minutes before turning out the layers onto the rack. Cool completely before finishing.

The baked layers may be stored tightly wrapped in plastic wrap at room temperature for 2 days. For longer storage, wrap tightly in plastic wrap and refrigerate for up to 5 days, or freeze wrapped in plastic wrap and then aluminum foil for up to 2 weeks. Do not unwrap before thawing.

TO MAKE THE FROSTING

1. In the bowl of an electric mixer fitted with the paddle attachment, combine the confectioners' sugar, butter, vanilla, and milk, and beat until light and fluffy, 2 to 3 minutes.

2. Add the peanut butter and mix until combined.

Use the frosting immediately, if possible. It may be stored in an airtight container at room temperature overnight, or in the refrigerator for up to 4 days. Let the frosting come to room temperature and briefly rebeat it in the mixer before using.

TO COMPLETE THE CAKE

See How to Assemble a Layer Cake (page 91) for instructions on how to fill and frost an unsplit layer cake. You will use the peanut butter frosting as the filling as well as the frosting. You might also try Coconut Pecan Frosting (page 103) as the filling and frosting for another great cake idea.

Serve the cake sliced at room temperature. It can be stored in a cake saver at room temperature for up to 3 days. For longer storage, wrap tightly in plastic wrap and refrigerate for up to 5 days. Just be sure to let it come to room temperature for best flavor before eating.

PRO TIP: When you mix the ingredients of the frosting, start on the lowest speed and turn on and off quickly a few times so the confectioners' sugar doesn't fly everywhere! When the ingredients come together, increase the speed to medium high.

COCONUT PECAN FROSTING

Feel like you've seen this frosting before? It's a traditional German chocolate cake frost-ing. It's so sweet and finger-licking gooey, I love it! I haven't made a German chocolate cake for my shop (yet!), but I love to slather this on the Devil's Food (page 100) and Classic Red Velvet (page 122) Cakes whenever possible. If you try it on the devil's food cake layers, you'll end up with a delicious cake that seems entirely unlike the Devil's Food Cake with Peanut Butter Frosting.

Makes 4 cups (enough to fill and frost one 9-inch cake)

One 12-ounce can evaporated milk
1½ cups sugar
5 slightly beaten large egg yolks
12 tablespoons unsalted butter
1½ teaspoons pure vanilla extract
½ teaspoon kosher salt
2 cups sweetened coconut flakes
2 cups pecan pieces, coarsely chopped

1. In a large saucepan over medium heat, combine the milk, sugar, egg yolks, butter, vanilla, and salt and cook, stirring constantly, until thickened, 10 to 13 minutes. Stir in the coconut and pecans.

2. Set aside to cool until thick enough to spread.

If not using immediately, refrigerate in an airtight container for up to 4 days.

SWEET ALMOND CAKE WITH LEMON CURD AND LEMON MASCARPONE FROSTING

I get very excited about this cake. The almond cake is deliriously delicious all on its own. To add thin layers of fresh lemon curd gilds the lily. But the silky, lemony mascarpone frosting? It's just too much (you should really try this—really).

Makes one 9-inch cake

FOR THE CAKE
2 cups sliced blanched almonds
2 cups sugar
1 cup all-purpose flour
1 teaspoon baking powder
¼ teaspoon salt
½ pound (2 sticks) unsalted butter
1½ teaspoons pure vanilla extract
¾ teaspoon almond extract
12 large egg whites, at room temperature

FOR THE LEMON CURD FILLING
3 large eggs
1 cup sugar
½ cup fresh lemon juice (about 5 lemons)
6 tablespoons unsalted butter

FOR THE LEMON MASCARPONE FROSTING
1¼ cups confectioners' sugar
Finely grated zest of 1 lemon
1 tablespoon fresh lemon juice
Pinch kosher salt
1¾ cups mascarpone cheese, at room temperature
12 tablespoons unsalted butter, at room temperature

BEFORE YOU START

Position a rack in the center of your oven. Preheat the oven to 350°F. Butter and flour two 9 × 2-inch round cake pans. Line each pan with a 9-inch round of parchment paper.

TO MAKE THE CAKE

1. In the bowl of a food processor fitted with the metal blade, combine the sliced almonds with ⅔ cup of the sugar and pulse grind until it is a coarse flour.

2. Transfer the almond flour to a large bowl. Add the all-purpose flour, an additional ⅔ cup of the sugar, the baking powder, and salt and whisk to combine.

3. Have ready a fine-meshed strainer. In a medium heavy-bottomed saucepan, brown the butter over medium heat. (The butter will melt first, and then the milk solids will settle to the bottom. After a little while, the milk solids will start to turn golden.) When the milk solids have reached a nutty brown color, immediately remove from the heat. Using the fine-meshed strainer, strain the butter into the flour mixture. Stir to combine. Discard the butter solids. Stir in the vanilla and almond extract.

4. In the very clean bowl of an electric mixer fitted with the very clean whip attachment, beat the egg whites on medium-high speed until they hold soft peaks. In a slow steady stream, with the mixer on medium, add the remaining ⅔ cup of the sugar. Increase the speed to high. Beat until there are firm—not dry—glossy peaks of meringue.

5. Using a rubber spatula, briskly fold one-third of the meringue mixture into the batter to lighten it. Gently fold in the remaining meringue until just combined.

6. Divide the batter evenly between the prepared pans. Spin the pans to level the batter. Bake for 25 to 30 minutes, or until a wooden skewer inserted into the center comes out clean. Remove to a wire rack to cool in the pans for 20 minutes before turning layers out onto the rack. Cool completely before filling or frosting.

The baked layers may be stored tightly wrapped in plastic wrap at room temperature for 2 days. For longer storage, wrap tightly in plastic wrap and refrigerate for up to 5 days, or freeze wrapped in plastic wrap and then aluminum foil for up to 2 weeks. Do not unwrap before thawing.

TO MAKE THE FILLING

1. In a medium nonreactive bowl, whisk together the eggs, sugar, lemon juice, and butter. Set the bowl over a pot of simmering, not boiling, water. Stir until the butter is melted. Continue to stir until the lemon curd thickens and is *nappante* (thick enough to coat the back of the spoon), about 10 minutes.

2. Strain the lemon curd into a clean bowl. Lay a sheet of plastic wrap flush against the surface of the lemon curd (to prevent a skin from forming). Place the bowl in an ice bath (see Note, page 99) to cool before using as a filling between layers. The curd will thicken upon cooling; use it only when cool. You will use about ⅔ cup of lemon curd for each layer.

The lemon curd keeps refrigerated in an airtight container for up to 1 week. Whisk until smooth before using.

TO MAKE THE FROSTING

1. In the bowl of an electric mixer fitted with the paddle attachment, combine the confectioners' sugar, zest, lemon juice, and salt on low speed until the sugar is dissolved.

2. Add the mascarpone and butter and mix until just combined. Do not overbeat or the frosting will be grainy. Rebeat briefly after standing, if needed.

The frosting keeps in an airtight container in the refrigerator for up to 4 days. Bring it to room temperature and beat briefly before using.

TO COMPLETE THE CAKE

See How to Assemble a Layer Cake (page 91) for instructions on how to fill and frost a split layer cake.

The cake is best eaten slightly chilled. it can be kept in a cake saver in the refrigerator for up to 3 days.

ROASTED PECAN CAKE WITH CARAMEL ORANGE MARMALADE AND BURNT ORANGE BUTTERCREAM

I made this cake for my friend Brandon's wedding, which was held in Virginia, at the beautiful farm where she grew up. She and I used to ride horses together, and Brandon loved to tell me of the adventures she'd had on her pony Irving back when she was a child—how they'd just take off for hours without a saddle or a plan.

When Brandon asked me to make her wedding cake, I wanted the decoration to capture the farm I imagined in my mind. She had a whimsical horsey cake topper that I embellished with fondant daisies. I decorated the rest of the cake to look like green pastures filled with lots of clover and lots of love. I only wish her pony could have had a slice.

Makes one 9-inch cake

FOR THE CAKE
1⅔ cups coarsely chopped pecan pieces, toasted (see Note, page 59) and cooled
2 cups sugar
1¼ cups all-purpose flour
1 teaspoon baking powder
½ teaspoon salt
½ pound (2 sticks) unsalted butter
2 teaspoons pure vanilla extract
12 large egg whites, at room temperature

FOR THE CARAMEL ORANGE MARMALADE
½ cup sugar
¼ cup water
3 tablespoons fresh orange juice
1 cup orange marmalade

FOR THE BURNT ORANGE BUTTERCREAM
¾ cup fresh orange juice
⅔ cup plus 3 tablespoons sugar
¼ cup water
3 large egg whites, at room temperature
¾ pound (3 sticks) unsalted butter, at room temperature
1 tablespoon pure vanilla extract

TO FINISH THE CAKE
1 cup pecan pieces, toasted (see Note, page 57)

Position a rack in the center of your oven. Preheat the oven to 350°F. Butter and flour two 9 × 2-inch round cake pans. Line each pan with a 9-inch round of parchment paper.

TO MAKE THE CAKE

1. In the bowl of a food processor fitted with the metal blade, combine the pecans with ⅔ cup of the sugar and pulse grind until it is a coarse pecan flour. Transfer to a large bowl. Add the all-purpose flour, an additional ⅔ cup of the sugar, the baking powder, and salt. Whisk to combine.

2. Have ready a fine-meshed strainer. In a medium heavy-bottomed saucepan, brown the butter over medium heat. (The butter will melt first, and then the milk solids will settle to the bottom. After a little while, the milk solids will start to turn golden.) When the milk solids have reached a nutty brown color, immediately remove from the heat.

3. Using the fine-meshed strainer, strain the butter into the flour mixture. Stir to combine. Discard the butter solids. Stir in the vanilla.

4. In the very clean bowl of an eletric mixer fitted with the very clean whip attachment, beat the egg whites on medium-high speed until they hold soft peaks. In a slow steady stream, with the mixer on medium speed, add the remaining ⅔ cup of the sugar and increase the speed back to high. Beat until there are firm—not dry— glossy peaks of meringue.

5. Using a rubber spatula, briskly fold one-third of the meringue mixture into the batter to lighten it. Add the remaining meringue and gently fold in until just combined.

6. Divide the batter evenly between the prepared pans. Spin the pans to level the batter. Bake for 25 minutes, or until a wooden skewer inserted into the center comes out clean. Remove to a wire rack to cool in the pans for 20 minutes before turning the layers out onto the rack. Cool completely before filling or frosting.

TO MAKE THE MARMALADE

1. In a small heavy-bottomed saucepan over medium heat, heat the sugar with the water until amber in color, like clover honey. Immediately remove from heat and stir in the orange juice to stop the cooking.

2. Add the marmalade and stir to combine. Set aside to cool.

The marmalade may be stored in an airtight container in the refrigerator for up to 2 weeks.

TO MAKE THE BUTTERCREAM

1. In a small heavy-bottomed saucepan over medium heat, reduce the orange juice until it is syrupy and just starts to caramelize (it turns brown). Watch it closely; don't let it burn! Add a splash of water to the caramel orange syrup to stop the cooking. Set aside to cool.

2. In another small heavy-bottomed saucepan over medium-high heat, combine the ⅔ cup of the sugar and water and cook to 240°F on a candy thermometer, about 7 minutes.

3. Meanwhile, in the bowl of an electric mixer fitted with the whip attachment, beat the egg whites on high speed until they hold soft peaks. Slowly add the 3 tablespoons sugar and beat until there are medium-stiff peaks of meringue.

4. When the sugar syrup reaches 240°F, decrease the speed of the mixer to medium, and immediately but slowly pour the hot liquid sugar in a steady stream down the side of the bowl and into the meringue. (Or, if the syrup is not yet 240°F when the meringue is ready, turn off the mixer until it is. Then turn on the mixer to medium and add the syrup.) Beat together until stiff glossy peaks form.

5. With the mixer still on medium, add the butter in pieces to the meringue. The mixture will break, but just keep beating and it will come together beautifully. Add the vanilla and reserved caramel orange syrup and mix to combine.

If using the buttercream immediately, set aside at room temperature. If not, refrigerate in an airtight container for up to 2 weeks. If the buttercream has been chilling, let it reach room temperature before beating it in the electric mixer. The buttercream will break, but then it will come together beautifully.

TO COMPLETE THE CAKE

1. See How to Assemble a Layer Cake (page 91) for instructions on how to fill and frost a split layer cake. You will split each cake layer in half, and spread one-third of the marmalade over each of the interior layers.

2. After frosting the cake, gently press the toasted pecans against the sides of the cake with your fingers.

This cake keeps very well, in a cake saver in the refrigerator for up to 5 days. The cake should come to room temperature before serving.

BROOKLYN BROWNOUT CAKE

Oh, this is a good one. It is a chocolate lover's fantasy, reminiscent of a chocolate mud cake. It may seem like a lot of steps, but really, it's just devil's food cake, brownies, and ganache—all things that are simple on their own. Make the brownies a few weeks ahead for some other occasion, and just snag four of them to pop in the freezer for when you are ready to make this cake. This cake is really worth it, and you'll see it's just not that difficult to do. **Makes one decadent 7-inch cake (serves up to 10 people)**

FOR THE CAKE
4 ounces best-quality unsweetened chocolate, coarsely chopped
½ cup vegetable or canola oil
2 cups sugar
1 cup plus 2 tablespoons all-purpose flour
3 tablespoons plus 1 teaspoon best-quality unsweetened Dutch-
  process cocoa powder
¾ teaspoon baking soda
½ teaspoon salt
½ cup sour cream
2 large eggs
¾ cup hot strong brewed coffee

FOR THE CHOCOLATE GANACHE FROSTING
12 ounces best-quality semisweet (58%) chocolate
1 cup heavy cream
2 tablespoons light corn syrup

FOR THE BROWNIE CRUMBLE
4 Chocolate Walnut Brownies (page 82)
¼ cup walnut pieces (optional)

BEFORE YOU START

Position a rack in the center of your oven. Preheat the oven to 350°F. Butter and flour two 7 × 2-inch round cake pans. Line each pan with a 7-inch round of parchment paper.

TO MAKE THE CAKE

1. In the top of a double boiler set over simmering, not boiling, water, melt the chocolate, stirring occasionally. When the chocolate is completely melted, whisk in the vegetable oil until smooth. Remove from the heat but keep warm over the hot water.

2. In the bowl of an electric mixer fitted with the paddle attachment, combine the sugar, flour, cocoa powder, baking soda, and salt, and mix well.

3. In a separate bowl, whisk together the sour cream and eggs until smooth.

4. Add the egg mixture to the flour mixture, and mix until combined. Be sure to scrape down the sides of the bowl. Add the melted chocolate mixture and mix until combined. Add the hot coffee in a stream, and mix until combined. (Again, scrape down the sides and bottom of the bowl.) The batter will be loose.

5. Divide the batter evenly between the prepared cake pans. Bake for 35 to 40 minutes, or until a wooden skewer inserted into the center comes out clean. Remove to a wire rack to cool in the pans for 25 minutes before turning out the layers onto the rack. Cool completely before finishing.

TO MAKE THE GANACHE

1. Chop the chocolate into small pieces and place in a medium bowl.

2. In a small saucepan over medium heat, bring the cream to scalding, or until the cream is steaming and tiny bubbles have formed along the edges.

3. Immediately pour the hot cream over the chocolate to cover completely. Do not stir. Wait 5 minutes, then whisk together until smooth. Stir in the corn syrup.

4. Lay a sheet of plastic wrap flush against the surface of the frosting. Let cool to slightly warm before using.

TO MAKE THE CRUMBLE AND COMPLETE THE CAKE

1. Trim the tops of the cake layers so that they are even and no longer domed (see page 91). Break the cake trimmings up into ¾- to 1-inch chunks and place in a medium bowl. Place one of the cake layers cut side up on a wire rack set over a cookie sheet lined with wax paper or parchment paper for glazing.

2. Break up the brownies into ¾- to 1-inch chunks. Combine the broken-up cake scraps with the brownie pieces. Pour half of the chocolate ganache over the brownies and cake scraps and stir gently with your fingers to coat. This is your brownie crumble.

3. Place one of the cake layers (cut side up) on a wire rack set over a cookie sheet lined with wax paper or parchment paper for glazing. Layer about ⅓ of the brownie crumble evenly over the top of the cake layer.

4. Place the remaining cake layer upside down on the other cake and press down gently with your hands.

5. Pour the remaining chocolate ganache over the assembled cake. Let it drip down over the sides of the cake. (You may use a metal offset spatula to help push some of the frosting from the top of the cake down the sides.) Spread the frosting with the spatula along the sides to seal. Don't worry if the separate layers are still visible. Once the frosting has stopped dripping, you may scrape up the excess that has dripped through the rack onto the paper and put it into the remaining brownie crumble (thou must not waste chocolate!).

CARROT CAKE WITH FRESH ORANGE CREAM CHEESE FROSTING

This is the cake I made for my little sister Erin's wedding. I made three square tiers and covered them in a baby blue fondant. Then I made "handkerchiefs" out of pure white fondant to drape over each layer, and I piped her favorite flower—lily of the valley—on the corner of each one. She and her husband, Rob, just loved it. She had 130 guests, and I baked enough cake for 200 people. It was all gone. It's very cool to be at a wedding and see people ask for seconds on the wedding cake—especially if you're the one who made it.

Makes one 8-inch cake

FOR THE CAKE
2 cups all-purpose flour
1½ tablespoons ground cinnamon
¾ teaspoon baking soda
¼ teaspoon baking powder
4 large eggs
¾ cup vegetable or canola oil
2 cups granulated sugar
1 teaspoon kosher salt
1 pound carrots, grated medium fine
¾ cup walnut pieces, coarsely chopped

FOR THE FRESH ORANGE CREAM CHEESE FROSTING
12 ounces cream cheese, softened
2½ cups confectioners' sugar
Zest of 1 orange
½ pound (2 sticks) unsalted butter, softened
1 teaspoon pure vanilla extract

BEFORE YOU START

Position a rack in the center of your oven. Preheat the oven to 350°F. Butter and flour two 8 × 2-inch round cake pans. Line each pan with an 8-inch round of parchment paper.

TO MAKE THE CAKE

1. In a medium bowl, whisk together the flour, cinnamon, baking soda, and baking powder.

2. In the bowl of an electric mixer fitted with the whip attachment, beat the eggs at high speed until light and frothy, about 1 minute. Decrease the speed to medium and add the oil, sugar, and salt, and mix until just combined. Decrease the speed to low and add the flour mixture, mixing until just combined.

3. Remove the bowl from the mixer. Using a rubber spatula, fold in the carrots and walnuts.

4. Divide the batter evenly between the prepared cake pans. Spin the pans to level the batter. Bake for 45 minutes, or until a wooden skewer inserted into the center comes out clean. Remove to a rack to cool for 20 minutes before turning the layers out onto the rack. Cool completely before filling or frosting.

The baked layers may be stored tightly wrapped at room temperature for 2 days. For longer storage, wrap tightly in plastic wrap and refrigerate for up to 5 days, or freeze wrapped in plastic wrap and then aluminum foil for up to 2 weeks. Do not unwrap before thawing.

TO MAKE THE FROSTING

1. In the bowl of an electric mixer fitted with the paddle attachment, combine the cream cheese, sugar, and zest. Start on low speed and then increase to medium-high speed and beat until smooth, 1½ to 2 minutes. Scrape down the sides of the bowl.

2. Add the butter and mix on medium speed until just fluffy and smooth, about 45 seconds more. Add the vanilla and mix until just combined. Do not overbeat.

TO COMPLETE THE CAKE

See How to Assemble a Layer Cake (page 91) for instructions on how to fill and frost an unsplit layer cake. You will use the fresh orange cream cheese frosting as both a filling and a frosting.

The cake keeps in a cake saver in the refrigerator for up to 4 days. It tastes great eaten at room temperature or chilled.

CHOCOLATE MALTED LAYER CAKE

When I was in grade school, my dad was the manager of Woolworth's on Twenty-third Street in New York City. At the very end of the summer, right before school started, I would go to work with him, so I could pick out all of the school supplies I'd need that year. It was something I looked forward to as much as Christmas morning. Aside from selecting an array of pretty pink and purple notebooks, sparkly pencils, coordinating binders and rainbow folders, I got to eat lunch at the soda fountain. The counter waitress would "keep an eye on me" as I ate my grilled cheese and tomato and drank my frosty chocolate malted. She would always give me the stainless steel blender cup filled with more malted to refill my glass when it was empty.

The chocolate malted is one of my most vivid flavor memories, and this cake instantly takes me back to sitting atop that twirly stool where my feet couldn't touch the floor.

Makes one 9-inch cake

FOR THE CAKE
6 ounces best-quality unsweetened chocolate, coarsely chopped
⅔ cup vegetable or canola oil
2⅔ cups sugar
1⅔ cups all-purpose flour
⅓ cup best-quality unsweetened Dutch-process cocoa powder
1 teaspoon baking soda
¾ teaspoon kosher salt
⅔ cup sour cream
3 large eggs
1⅓ cups hot strong brewed coffee

FOR THE CHOCOLATE MALTED FROSTING
1 pound best-quality milk (38%) chocolate
1 cup heavy cream
1 cup malted milk powder
¼ cup light corn syrup
8 tablespoons (1 stick) unsalted butter, at room temperature (not warm)
8 ounces malted milk balls

BEFORE YOU START

Position a rack in the center of your oven. Preheat the oven to 350°F. Butter and flour two 9 × 2-inch round cake pans. Line each pan with a 9-inch round of parchment paper.

TO MAKE THE CAKE

1. In the top of a double boiler set over simmering, not boiling, water, melt the chocolate, stirring occasionally. When the chocolate is completely melted, whisk in the vegetable oil until smooth. Remove from the heat, but keep warm over the hot water.

2. In the bowl of an electric mixer fitted with the paddle attachment, combine the sugar, flour, cocoa powder, baking soda, and salt, and mix well.

3. In a separate bowl, whisk together the sour cream and eggs until smooth.

4. Add the egg mixture to the flour mixture, and mix until combined. Be sure to scrape down the sides of the the bowl. Add the melted chocolate mixture and mix until combined. Add the hot coffee in a stream, and mix until combined. (Again, scrape down the sides and bottom of the bowl.) The batter will be loose.

5. Divide the batter evenly between the prepared cake pans. Bake for 35 to 40 minutes, or until a wooden skewer inserted into the center comes out clean. Remove to a wire rack to cool in the pans for 25 minutes before turning out the layers onto the rack. Cool completely before finishing.

The baked layers may be stored tightly wrapped at room temperature for 2 days. For longer storage, wrap tightly in plastic wrap and refrigerate for up to 5 days, or freeze wrapped in plastic wrap and then aluminum foil for up to 2 weeks. Do not unwrap before thawing.

TO MAKE THE FROSTING

1. Chop the chocolate into small pieces and place in a medium bowl.

2. In a small saucepan over medium heat, bring cream to scalding, or until the cream is steaming and tiny bubbles have formed along the edges. Whisk in the malt powder to combine. Pour over the chocolate to cover completely. Do not stir. Wait 5 minutes, then whisk until creamy. Stir in the corn syrup. Lay a sheet of plastic wrap flush against the surface of the frosting. Let cool to room temperature.

3. When the chocolate is cooled, place it in the bowl of an electric mixer fitted with the paddle attachment. Add the butter one tablespoon at a time and mix on low speed until smooth. (If the frosting is too loose to spread, chill briefly and stir occasionally until it is a nice spreading consistency.)

TO COMPLETE THE CAKE

1. See How to Assemble a Layer Cake (page 91) for instructions on how to fill and frost an unsplit layer cake. You will use the chocolate malted frosting as both the filling and the frosting.

2. Once the cake is frosted, place the malted milk balls on top of the cake.

This cake is best served at room temperature, but it can be kept in a cake saver in the refrigerator for up to 5 days. Bring to room temperature before serving.

HAZELNUT RASPBERRY LAYER CAKE

This is a very elegant (it's pink!) cake for any special occasion. Eat it at room temperature because buttercream just isn't as yummy when it's cold. If you've had it in the refrigerator, be sure to let the cake sit out of the fridge for at least one hour before serving.

Makes one 9-inch cake

FOR THE CAKE
1⅔ cups hazelnuts or filberts, toasted (see Note, page 59) and
  cooled
2 cups sugar
1 cup all-purpose flour
1 teaspoon baking powder
½ pound (2 sticks) unsalted butter
2 teaspoons pure vanilla extract
12 large egg whites, at room temperature

FOR THE RASPBERRY BUTTERCREAM
1 cup loosely packed fresh raspberries
2 tablespoons raspberry liqueur
⅔ cup plus 3 tablespoons sugar
¼ cup water
3 large egg whites, at room temperature
¾ pound (3 sticks) unsalted butter, at room temperature
1⅓ cups seedless raspberry preserves, for filling
2 cups fresh raspberries, for garnish

BEFORE YOU START

Position a rack in the center of your oven. Preheat the oven to 350°F. Butter and flour two 9 × 2-inch cake pans. Line each pan with a 9-inch round of parchment paper.

TO MAKE THE CAKE

1. In the bowl of a food processor fitted with the metal blade, combine the hazelnuts with ⅔ cup of the sugar and pulse grind until it is a coarse flour.

2. Transfer the hazelnut flour to a large bowl. Add the all-purpose flour, an additional ⅔ cup of the sugar, and the baking powder, and whisk to combine.

3. Have ready a fine-meshed strainer. In a medium heavy-bottomed saucepan, brown the butter over medium heat. (The butter will melt first, and then the milk solids will settle to the bottom. After a little while, the milk solids will start to turn golden.) When the milk solids have reached a nutty brown color, immediately remove from the heat. Using the fine-meshed strainer, strain the butter into the flour mixture. Stir to combine. Discard the butter solids. Stir in the vanilla.

4. In the very clean bowl of an electric mixer fitted with the very clean whip attachment, beat the egg whites on medium-high speed until they hold soft peaks. In a slow steady stream, with the mixer on medium speed, add the remaining ⅔ cup of the sugar. Increase the speed to high. Beat until there are firm—not dry—glossy peaks of meringue.

5. Using a rubber spatula, briskly fold one-third of the meringue into the batter to lighten it. Add the remaining meringue and gently fold in until just combined.

6. Divide the batter evenly between the prepared cake pans. Spin the pans or use an offset spatula to level the batter. Bake for 25 to 30 minutes, or until a wooden skewer inserted into the center comes out clean. Remove to a wire rack to cool in the pans for 20 minutes before turning the layers out onto the rack. Cool completely before filling or frosting.

The baked layers may be stored tightly wrapped at room temperature for 2 days. For longer storage, wrap tightly in plastic wrap and refrigerate for up to 5 days, or freeze wrapped in plastic wrap and then aluminum foil for up to 2 weeks. Do not unwrap before thawing.

TO MAKE THE BUTTERCREAM

1. In a small bowl, combine the fresh raspberries with the raspberry liqueur.

2. In a small heavy-bottomed saucepan over medium-high heat, combine the ⅔ cup of sugar and the water and cook to 240°F on a candy thermometer, about 7 minutes.

3. Meanwhile, in the bowl of an electric mixer fitted with the whip attachment, beat the egg whites on high speed until they hold soft peaks. Slowly add the 3 tablespoons sugar and beat until there are medium stiff—but not dry—peaks of meringue.

4. When the sugar syrup reaches 240°F, decrease the speed of the mixer to medium, and immediately but slowly pour the hot liquid sugar in a steady stream down the side of the bowl and into the meringue. (Or, if the syrup is not yet 240°F when the meringue is ready, turn off the mixer until it is. Then turn on the mixer to medium and add the syrup.) Beat together until stiff glossy peaks form.

5. With the mixer on medium speed, add the butter in pieces to the meringue. The mixture will break, but just keep beating and it will come together beautifully.

6. Pour the raspberries and the raspberry liquid into the buttercream and beat on medium-high speed until combined.

If using the buttercream immediately, set aside at room temperature. If not, refrigerate in an airtight container for up to 2 weeks. If the buttercream has been chilled, let it reach room temperature before beating it in the electric mixer. The buttercream will break, but then it will come together beautifully.

TO COMPLETE THE CAKE

1. See How to Assemble a Layer Cake (page 91) for instructions on how to fill and frost a split layer cake. You will use the raspberry preserves as the filling.

2. After frosting the cake, garnish the top of the cake with the fresh raspberries. If you are making the cake a few days ahead, finish the cake to the point that it is frosted, but wait to buy the berries and put them on the cake until the day you will be serving it. You want the fruit to be fresh as possible.

3. Let the cake sit at room temperature for at least 1 hour before serving.

This cake keeps very well in a cake saver at room temperature for 2 days. For longer storage, store in a cake saver in the refrigerator for up to 4 days. It should come to room temperature before serving.

CLASSIC RED VELVET CAKE WITH CREAM CHEESE FROSTING

This cake has a bit of cocoa and cinnamon for flavor, buttermilk and vinegar for rich-ness and tang, and red food coloring for . . . what? This cake was traditionally flavored with beet juice, which gave it its luscious red hue. Now natural food colorings are avail-able, which are lots of fun to experiment with (but the blue and green may turn your tongue funny colors!).

Makes one 9-inch cake

FOR THE CAKE
3¾ cups all-purpose flour
3 tablespoons best-quality unsweetened Dutch-process cocoa
  powder
2 teaspoons ground cinnamon
1½ teaspoons baking soda
1 teaspoon salt
1½ cups buttermilk
1½ teaspoons pure vanilla extract
2¼ cups sugar
1½ cups vegetable or canola oil
3 large eggs
1½ teaspoons red wine vinegar
2 teaspoons natural red food coloring

FOR THE CLASSIC CREAM CHEESE FILLING AND FROSTING
12 ounces cream cheese, softened
3 cups confectioners' sugar
¾ pound (3 sticks) unsalted butter, softened
2 teaspoons pure vanilla extract

BEFORE YOU START

Position a rack in the center of your oven. Preheat the oven to 350°F. Butter and flour two 9 × 2-inch round cake pans. Line each pan with a 9-inch round of parchment paper.

TO MAKE THE CAKE

1. In a medium bowl, whisk together the flour, cocoa powder, cinnamon, baking soda, and salt until combined.

2. In a small bowl, whisk together the buttermilk and vanilla.

3. In the bowl of an electric mixer fitted with the whip attachment, cream the sugar and oil. Add the eggs and beat well. Add the vinegar and food coloring and mix to combine.

4. Add the flour mixture to the batter in three batches, alternating with the buttermilk mixture. Mix well after each addition. Scrape down the sides of the bowl. Beat well for 10 more seconds.

5. Divide the batter evenly between the prepared cake pans. Spin the pans to level the batter. Bake for 35 to 40 minutes, or until a wooden skewer inserted into the center comes out clean. Remove to a wire rack to cool for 20 minutes before turning the layers out onto the rack. Cool completely before filling or frosting.

The baked layers may be stored tightly wrapped at room temperature for 3 days. For longer storage, wrap tightly in plastic wrap and refrigerate for up to 5 days, or freeze wrapped in plastic wrap and then aluminum foil for up to 2 weeks. Do not unwrap before thawing.

TO MAKE THE FROSTING

1. In the bowl of an electric mixer fitted with the paddle attachment, combine the cream cheese and confectioners' sugar. Start on low speed to combine, and then continue on medium-high speed until just fluffy and smooth, 1½ to 2 minutes. Scrape down the sides of the bowl.

2. Add the butter and vanilla and mix until just combined, about 45 seconds more. Do not overbeat. Use immediately.

TO COMPLETE THE CAKE

See How to Assemble a Layer Cake (page 91) for instructions on how to fill and frost an unsplit layer cake. You will use the cream cheese frosting as a filling and a frosting.

Serve the cake at room temperature. It keeps well in a cake saver at room temperature for 2 days, or in the refrigerator for up to 5 days.

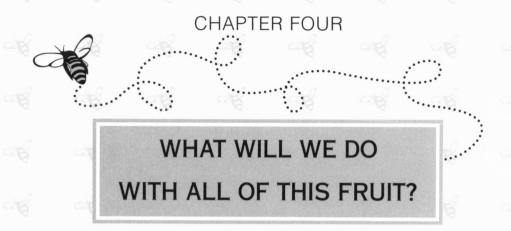

CHAPTER FOUR

WHAT WILL WE DO WITH ALL OF THIS FRUIT?

Fresh Fruit Pies, Cobblers, Crumbles, and Preserves

Strawberry Shortcakes

A Lesson on Pie Dough

Flaky Pie Dough

All-Butter Pie Dough

Sweet Dough for Pies, Tarts, and Sugar Cookies

Strawberry Rhubarb Cobbler Pie

Sour Cherry Pie with Pistachio Crumble

Pear Cranberry Pie with Gingersnap Crumble

North Fork Peach Raspberry Pie

Cherry Clafoutis Tart

Bear's Peach Cobbler

Double-Crusted Caramel Apple Pie

Lemon Blueberry Buttermilk Pie

Apple Orchard Pecan Crumble

Plum Raspberry Pie with a Sweet Almond Lattice

Master Recipe for Preserves

Cinnamon Peach Preserves

Plum Raspberry Preserves

Strawberry Rhubarb Preserves with Fresh Orange

Jumbleberry Preserves

Strawberry–Ruby Grapefruit Preserves

Pick Your Own

MY FAMILY HAD just finished an early dinner, and I was running toward the car while trying to tie my sneakers at the same time. It was near the end of June in 1976 and strawberry season had arrived in our small town in upstate New York. My anticipation had grown throughout the day, as my mom and I prepared for the evening's event. We'd bought a carton of fresh cream for whipping, and we'd read her dog-eared copy of *Fanny Farmer* that explained once more how to cut cold butter into flour and sugar. When we returned from the farm that evening, we would eat the first of the season's strawberry shortcakes.

Picking started at 5:00 p.m., when the sun's intensity had begun to wane. As we pulled into a dirt drive, I recognized the peeling paint of the old white farmhouse and recalled the previous year when I had

waited impatiently on its wraparound porch for my big brothers to return with their treasure. I could barely contain my excitement as I ran to the makeshift stand where the baskets were piled up alongside a huge rusty old scale. I smiled proudly as an old wrinkled woman asked, "Are you five years old?"

I was. This was the first year I was trusted not to trample on the beautiful plants. I gingerly led the way into the vast strawberry patch, and started to fill my basket with the most handsome red berries. "Go ahead, you can eat one," my mom informed me. I plucked a giant scarlet beauty into my little mouth, and its sweet juices dripped down my chin. Now this was worth the five-year wait.

When the little thorns had pricked us enough, and our lips and fingers were sufficiently berry stained, it was time to weigh in and go home to the shortcakes and a week's worth of jamming. Mom and I would make enough strawberry jam to last us throughout the fall and winter months. When we'd start to run low, it would be late June, and time to go picking again.

At my shop, Sweet Melissa Pâtisserie, I use strawberries for more than just shortcakes. The fragrant berries find their way into a variety of pies, tarts, and muffins. Luckily, the berries are shipped in from all

Sweet Plum Clafoutis with Almonds (page 30)

Bee Stings *(page 47)*

Chocolate Chip Cookies with Toasted Almonds *(page 58)*

Chestnut Honey Madeleines *(page 62)*

Fluffy Coconut Cake with Passion Fruit Filling *(page 96)*

Strawberry Shortcake *(page 130)*

Sour Cherry Pie with Pistachio Crumble *(page 146)*

Sweet Almond Bread Pudding with Raspberry Sauce *(page 174)*

over the world, from warm places like Chile and California, and are available most months of the year. But in my opinion, the very best berries still arrive locally at the end of June. When the season comes, I borrow a friend's truck, bring along my mom and sister, and get down to some serious picking. We need to make tons of strawberry jam to serve with all of our scones and fresh croissants. Sometimes I add a bit of rhubarb, or a touch of orange zest, and my mom approves of them all!

I always set aside the very best berries for shortcakes, and we serve up plenty of them at the shop and at home. I still loosely follow *Fannie Farmer*'s recipe, but I've added a bit of sugar, some freshly grated lemon zest, and cream to hold it all together. The Strawberry Shortcakes on page 130 taste just as good as I remember, and when the local berries are ripe, it is always one of my favorites.

STRAWBERRY SHORTCAKES

Makes 6 shortcakes

FOR THE SHORTCAKES
2 cups all-purpose flour
2 teaspoons baking powder
½ teaspoon kosher salt
2 tablespoons sugar plus 1 tablespoon for glazing
1 teaspoon freshly grated lemon zest
4 tablespoons (½ stick) cold unsalted butter,
  cut into ¼-inch pieces
1 cup cold heavy cream
2 tablespoons whole milk or heavy cream, for glazing

FOR THE STRAWBERRIES
1 dry quart fresh strawberries, rinsed, hulled, and sliced
3 tablespoons sugar (or more to your taste)

FOR THE WHIPPED CREAM
1 cup cold heavy cream
¾ teaspoon pure vanilla extract
1 tablespoon plus 1½ teaspoons sugar

BEFORE YOU START

Position a rack in the center of your oven. Preheat the oven to 350°F. Line a cookie sheet with parchment paper or aluminum foil.

TO MAKE THE SHORTCAKES

1. In a large bowl, whisk together the flour, baking powder, salt, 2 tablespoons of the sugar, and the zest. Using a pastry blender, cut in the butter until it resembles a coarse meal. Little by little, stir in heavy cream until the dough starts to hold together (you may use a bit more cream if need be).

2. Turn the dough out onto a lightly floured work surface. Pat together to form a rect-angle 5 inches wide by 7½ inches long that is about 1 inch thick. Cut the long side

of the dough into thirds, and the width in half to form six 2½-inch squares. Place the shortcakes 3 inches apart on the prepared cookie sheet.

3. Brush the tops of the shortcakes with the milk or heavy cream and sprinkle with the remaining tablespoon of sugar. Bake for 20 to 25 minutes, or until light golden brown. Remove to a wire rack to cool to room temperature.

While the shortcakes are cooling, prepare the strawberries. In a medium bowl, combine the sliced strawberries with the sugar. Set aside for 20 to 30 minutes to macerate.

TO MAKE THE WHIPPED CREAM

In the bowl of an electric mixer fitted with the whip attachment, beat the heavy cream and vanilla on medium speed. In a slow steady stream, add the sugar and beat until the mixture forms medium-stiff peaks.

The whipped cream is best used when just made, but can be refrigerated in an airtight container overnight and beaten again before serving.

TO COMPLETE THE SHORTCAKES

Fork split each shortcake in half horizontally. Place one half on each of six plates. Spoon 2 tablespoons of berries on each. Top each with a large dollop of whipped cream. Spoon more berries on top. Place each of the remaining halves on top of the berries. Garnish with more cream and berries, if desired. Add a sprig of mint for garnish, if you'd like.

PRO TIP: When whipping cream, the colder the cream the better. If the bowl, the whisk or beaters, and the heavy cream are all well chilled, you will achieve the most volume.

Prepare the strawberries and whipped cream no more than 30 minutes before serving. The shortcakes are best eaten the day they are made, but they can be tightly wrapped in plastic wrap and then aluminum foil and frozen for up to 3 weeks. Do not unwrap before defrosting.

FOR ALL OF the single-crusted pies with *non*prebaked crusts, the dough should be rolled, fitted into the pie plate, edge crimped, and refrigerated for 30 minutes before filling.

The oven should be preheated before making the filling, *not* before rolling the dough (see page 138).

A Lesson on Pie Dough

PIE DOUGH CONTINUES to be one of the most daunting aspects of most cooks' repertoires. Lucky for me, I was started on it early and never learned to fear it. I do, however, find it can be temperamental if you don't take it seriously. In experimenting with different fat ratios and temperatures, I learned what you don't want to create: either a dough that is too tender and "sandy" tasting, and therefore impossible to roll (a result of overworking the fat into the flour), or a dough that is tough and not at all flaky (a result of working in too much flour or water and overrolling the dough and therefore overdeveloping its gluten). The rules for making pie dough are simple, but they must be respected. If you follow the directions here you will make a beautiful pie crust.

Before we make the dough, let's talk about the short list of ingre-

dients: flour, salt, butter, shortening, and water. Nothing difficult about that. The only secret here is to be sure that all of your ingredients are cold.

FLOUR

I'm using all-purpose flour in my recipe. Some timid bakers may want to use cake or pastry flour, because they're afraid of gluten. You can if you want to—just swap it in for the all-purpose flour here. But I don't think it's necessary, and I prefer the structure that the all-purpose flour lends to the dough. Chilling the flour will also help make the process easier and more successful. Measure the flour out into a medium mixing bowl (the same bowl in which you will be making your dough), throw the tablespoon of salt on top, and pop it in the freezer.

BUTTER

Now butter has to be really cold. Start with cold unsalted butter from the refrigerator, measure out what you need, and then cut it lengthwise in half, and then turn it on its side and cut lengthwise. Cut once through the center, creating two halves; then cut each half through the center, then each of those little halves through the center. Try to make all of the pieces the same size. This might sound complicated, but you're just making small equal-size pieces of butter! Put them in a bowl and pop the bowl in the freezer, too.

SHORTENING

I think it's smart to store shortening in the freezer so it is always cold and ready to be made into pie dough. To use it, measure out what you need, put it in a little bowl, and put the bowl in the freezer.

WATER

You can use cold water from the tap (if you have good-tasting water) or bottled is fine, too. Either way the water must be cold. So throw in a few ice cubes and pull them out before you add it to the dough. How much water you'll add is the only variable. If it's raining outside, you'll need less, up to two tablespoons less. You'll add it a bit at a time and check it as you go. The water just needs to bring the dough together.

So now you know the importance of keeping the ingredients cold. It's time for the technique.

TECHNIQUE

My favorite method for making pie dough is by hand, using a metal pastry blender. If you don't have one, get one. It is not expensive, and you'll use it every time you make this dough. As an added bonus, kids *love* using a pastry blender—and it keeps their hot little fingers out of the flour! Some cooks may want to use their food processors, an electric mixer, their fingers, or two butter knives for cutting the butter and shortening into the flour. You can play around with any of these methods—*after* you learn to use the pastry blender. When you use the pastry blender, you have a more intimate relationship with the dough. You can watch it as it changes, gain an understanding of how it works, and learn to tell when it's just right. This will help you learn what to look for *before* you try other techniques

One other thing to remember: You need to work quickly, always trying to maintain the cold temperature of your ingredients. Pull things from the freezer when you need them and not before. If your mom calls, put everything back in the freezer.

FLAKY PIE DOUGH

My favorite recipe is based on one of the great Julia Child recipes. It uses both butter (for flavor) and shortening (for flakiness).

Makes enough for 1 double-crust or 2 single-crust 10-inch pies

2¾ cups all-purpose flour
½ teaspoon salt
5 tablespoons cold unsalted butter, cut into ½-inch pieces
½ cup plus 2 tablespoons cold vegetable shortening
6 to 8 tablespoons ice water

TO MAKE THE DOUGH

1. Before you start, see "A Lesson on Pie Dough" (page 133). Take the flour/salt bowl from the freezer. Whisk together. Take the butter from the freezer and, using your hands, quickly drop each piece separately into the flour mixture (don't hold a lot of them in your hand at one time or you'll melt them). Every now and then using your fingers toss the butter pieces into the flour so that each piece of cold butter is covered with flour.

2. Using a pastry blender, cut the butter into the flour until the butter is the size of large peas. (Using a pastry blender is easy. Just put it into the shortening and push through while slightly rotating the blender a quarter spin, which cuts and blends in the same operation. Repeat as needed to obtain a good blend or crumbly mixture. You do occasionally have to clear or remove ingredients that stick to the side of the pastry blender and a butter knife works well for this.)

3. Now, take the shortening from the freezer and, using your fingertips, scoop out little pieces and toss them into the flour with your fingers as you go (just like you did with the butter chunks).

4. Using the pastry blender, cut the shortening into the flour mixture until the shortening and the butter are the size of medium to small peas.

5. Now, the water. If you added any ice cubes to the water, pull them out now. Make a well in the center of the flour mixture with your fingers. Pour half of the ice-cold water into the well. Use a fork to gently pull the flour from the sides of the bowl into the well.

Keep turning the bowl and pulling the flour in. The dough should start to come together. Now, add half of the remaining water and continue to pull toward the middle. When the dough has enough water, it will hold together when you squeeze it in the palm of your hand. If it is holding together, stop. If it is not quite there yet, add the remaining water and toss until it does.

6. Turn the dough out onto a lightly floured work surface. Pat it together into one piece. Divide the dough into two equal parts, flatten each into a round disk, and then wrap tightly in plastic wrap. Refrigerate for at least 45 minutes. Put what you will use today in the fridge, and the rest (if there is any) goes in the freezer for another time.

TO ROLL THE DOUGH

1. When the dough is chilled through, lightly flour a work surface. Unwrap the dough disk, lightly flour the top, and, using a rolling pin, press gently on the dough, from the middle upward, and then the middle downward. Turn the dough disk a quarter turn and repeat the light pressing process. Add more flour if needed to prevent sticking.

2. The dough should now be a round, flatter version of the original dough disk. Sprinkle lightly with more flour if necessary, then gently roll the dough so that it is an inch wider all around than it was. Make a quarter turn, lifting the dough if it is sticking and lightly flouring the work surface below. Repeat this process until the round is roughly 12 inches in diameter and ¼ inch thick. Slide it onto a cookie sheet lined with parchment or wax paper and chill it in the fridge until you are ready to prebake or assemble your pie.

3. When you are ready to bake the dough, transfer it to a pie plate by sliding both palms under the dough and gently lifting it and placing it down over the center of the pie plate. Gently press the dough into the pie plate, being careful not to stretch it. Patch any rips or tears by pressing the dough together with your fingers.

4. Using clean scissors, trim off any dough in excess of 1½ inches around the edges. Then gently roll the dough's edge under itself, creating a nice uniform edge to crimp. Lightly flour a fork and press the tines along the top of the folded edge all around, or pinch the dough all around between your index finger and your thumb.

5. Put the piecrust in the refrigerator to rest and chill for at least 30 minutes.

TO PREBAKE OR BLIND BAKE THE CRUST

Some pies call for a crust that is prebaked or blind baked. These pies usually have a very liquidy filling, and when filled, will not stay in the oven more than 45 minutes or so. Because of the liquid filling and the relatively short cooking time, the crust will not have a chance to properly bake. That's why these crusts on these pies need to be prebaked.

1. Position a rack in the bottom third of your oven. Preheat the oven to 350°F. Line the prepared piecrust with parchment paper or lightly greased aluminum foil, and then fill it with pie weights. I like to use dried lentils for blind baking, but you may also use dried rice or beans. (Just don't use popcorn kernels!)

2. Bake for 25 to 30 minutes, or until, upon lifting the liner, the crust appears "dry" and no longer has the look of raw dough. Remove the weights and liner and continue to bake for an additional 10 to 15 minutes, or until the crust is lightly golden. Remove to a wire rack to cool before adding the filling.

TRY IT WITH A TWIST: Try adding ½ teaspoon lemon zest and ¼ teaspoon ground cinnamon to the flour and salt mixture. It gives the crust a wonderful flavor, especially for fruit pies.

ALL-BUTTER PIE DOUGH

All-Butter Pie Dough bakes up more crisp than the Flaky Pie Dough (page 137) and is great for pumpkin pie, pecan pie, as well as fruit pies. It has a rich buttery flavor.

Makes enough dough for 1 double-crusted pie or 2 single-crust 10-inch pies

2¼ cups all-purpose flour
2 tablespoons sugar
¼ teaspoon baking powder
½ teaspoon kosher salt
1 cup very cold unsalted butter, cut into ½-inch pieces
6 to 8 tablespoons ice water

TO MAKE THE DOUGH BY HAND

1. In a large bowl, whisk together the flour, sugar, baking powder, and salt to combine.

2. Add the butter pieces, tossing with your fingers to coat each cube in the flour. Using a pastry blender, cut the butter into the flour until it is the size of large peas. (See Flaky Pie Dough step 2 on page 137 for instruction on using a pastry blender.)

3. Sprinkle 6 tablespoons of the water over the mixture and toss with a fork. The dough should hold together when you squeeze it in your hand. If it is too dry, add the rest of the water (or more if absolutely necessary).

TO MAKE THE DOUGH USING A FOOD PROCESSOR

1. In the bowl of a food processor fitted with the metal blade, pulse flour, sugar, baking powder, and salt to combine.

2. Add the butter pieces, carefully tossing with your fingers to coat each one in flour. Pulse briefly, until the butter is the size of large peas.

3. Add 6 tablespoons of the water and pulse to combine. The dough should just hold together when you squeeze it in your hand. If it is too dry, add the rest of the of water (or more if absolutely necessary).

TO REST AND ROLL THE DOUGH

1. Turn the dough out onto a lightly floured work surface. Pat it together into one piece. Divide the dough into two equal parts, flatten each into a round disk, and then wrap tightly in plastic wrap. Refrigerate for at least 30 minutes before rolling.

2. To roll, follow the instructions on page 138.

SWEET DOUGH FOR PIES, TARTS, AND SUGAR COOKIES

This is a basic sugar cookie dough that is wonderful when rolled thin and used for pies and tarts.

Makes enough dough for two 9- or 10-inch tarts or approximately two dozen 2½-inch cutouts

14 tablespoons unsalted butter, at room temperature
½ cup sugar
Freshly grated zest of ½ lemon
½ teaspoon kosher salt
1 large egg
½ teaspoon pure vanilla extract
2 cups all-purpose flour

TO MAKE THE DOUGH

1. In the bowl of an electric mixer fitted with the paddle attachment, cream the butter, sugar, zest, and salt until light and fluffy, about 2 minutes.

2. Add the egg and vanilla and mix to combine.

3. Add the flour and mix to combine. Be sure to scrape down the bowl.

4. Turn the dough out onto a lightly floured work suface. Pat it together into one piece. Divide the dough into two equal parts, flatten into 6-inch round disks, and wrap tightly in plastic wrap. Put what you will use today in the fridge, and the rest (if there is any) goes in the freezer for another time. Chill for at least 45 minutes before rolling.

TO ROLL THE DOUGH

1. When the dough is chilled through, remove it from the refrigerator and let it rest at room temperature for 10 minutes, until it is malleable. Lightly flour a work surface. Begin with one dough disk, lightly flour the top, and, using a rolling pin, press gently on the dough from the middle upward, and then the middle downward. Turn the dough disk a quarter turn and repeat the light pressing process. Add more flour if needed to prevent sticking.

2. The dough should now be a round, flatter version of the original dough disk. Sprinkle lightly with more flour if necessary, and gently roll the dough so that it is an inch wider all around than it was. Make a quarter turn, lifting the dough if it is sticking and lightly flouring the work surface below. Repeat this process until the round is roughly 12 inches in diameter and ¼ inch thick.

3. Place the dough in the pie plate or tart pan and press lightly to fit. Do not stretch the dough to fit. Instead, push the dough with your fingers until it is in place. Using clean scissors, trim the edge of the crust so that there is ½ inch of dough hanging over the edges. Turn the excess dough under itself, creating a nice uniform edge to crimp. If you have any cracks or holes, simply patch them by pressing the dough together with your fingers. Refrigerate until firm, 20 to 30 minutes.

TO PREBAKE THE CRUST

1. Position a rack in the bottom third of your oven. Preheat the oven to 350°F. Line the piecrust with parchment paper or lightly greased aluminum foil, and then fill it to the top with pie weights. I like to use dried lentils for blind baking, but you may also use dried rice or beans. (Just don't use popcorn kernels!)

2. Bake for 30 to 35 minutes, or until, upon lifting the liner, the crust appears "dry" and no longer has the appearance of raw dough. Remove the weights and liner. If the edges are getting very brown, lightly tent with aluminum foil. Bake for an additional 10 to 15 minutes, or until the crust is lightly golden. Remove to a wire rack to cool before adding the filling.

STRAWBERRY RHUBARB COBBLER PIE

Ooooo, I love the idea of cobbler pie—buttery sweet biscuits on top of bubbling fruit, all inside a flaky piecrust. Top with Brown Sugar Vanilla Ice Cream (page 183) for pure heaven.

Makes one 9-inch pie

FOR THE PIECRUST
½ recipe for Flaky Pie Dough (page 137)

FOR THE COBBLER TOPPING
1 cup all-purpose flour
1 teaspoon baking powder
¼ teaspoon kosher salt
2 tablespoons sugar plus 1½ teaspoons, for sprinkling
½ teaspoon freshly grated lemon zest
2 tablespoons cold unsalted butter, cut into ¼-inch pieces
½ cup heavy cream, chilled
1 tablespoon whole milk or heavy cream, for glazing

FOR THE STRAWBERRY RHUBARB FILLING
2 cups rinsed, hulled, and sliced fresh strawberries (¼-inch
  slices)
2 cups cleaned and sliced fresh rhubarb (½-inch slices)
1 tablespoon fresh lemon juice
1½ cups sugar
2 tablespoons cornstarch

TO PREPARE THE PIECRUST

Roll out the dough into a round 12 inches wide and ¼ inch thick. Gently fit it into a 9-inch pie plate. Fold the edges under and crimp. Refrigerate until firm, about 30 minutes.

TO MAKE THE COBBLER TOPPING

1. In a large bowl, whisk together the flour, baking powder, salt, the 2 tablespoons sugar, and zest. Using a pastry blender, cut in the butter until it resembles a coarse

meal. Little by little, stir in the heavy cream until the dough starts to hold together (a bit more cream may be used if need be).

2. Turn the dough out onto a lightly floured work surface. Pat together to form a round that is ½ inch thick. Using a lightly floured 2½-inch round biscuit cutter, cut the dough into 7 or 8 biscuits.

3. Place the biscuits on the prepared cookie sheet and refrigerate, loosely covered with plastic wrap, until ready to use.

BEFORE YOU MAKE THE FILLING

Position a rack in the bottom third of your oven. Preheat the oven to 350°F. Line a cookie sheet with parchment paper or aluminum foil.

TO MAKE THE FILLING

1. In a medium bowl, combine the strawberries, rhubarb, lemon juice, sugar, and cornstarch and mix gently.

2. Pour the fruit mixture into the unbaked pie shell.

TO COMPLETE THE PIE

1. Place the cobbler biscuits evenly on top of the strawberry mixture. Brush with the milk and sprinkle with some of the 1½ teaspoons of sugar.

2. Place the pie plate on the freshly lined cookie sheet. Bake for about 1 hour and 15 minutes, or until the juices are bubbling and thick. (To check the "doneness" of the biscuits, carefully lift one to see that the bottom looks like a steamed "dumpling" and not raw dough.) Remove to a wire rack to cool to room temperature before serving.

Fresh fruit pies are best eaten the day they are baked.

SOUR CHERRY PIE WITH PISTACHIO CRUMBLE

My talented friend Andrea Lekberg created this pie during her tenure as pastry chef at Sweet Melissa's. Lucky for us! It is my favorite pie, and one of the best-selling pies at the shops.

Makes one 10-inch pie

FOR THE PIECRUST
½ recipe Flaky Pie Dough (page 137)

FOR THE PISTACHIO CRUMBLE
½ cup all-purpose flour
⅔ cup whole oats, ground to a flour in a food processor (yielding ½ cup oat flour)
½ cup sugar
½ teaspoon ground cinnamon
½ teaspoon kosher salt
¾ cup shelled unsalted whole pistachios, coarsely ground in a food processor or chopped medium fine by hand
6 tablespoons unsalted butter, melted and cooled

FOR THE SOUR CHERRY FILLING
¾ cup sugar
3 tablespoons cornstarch
¼ teaspoon kosher salt
2¼ pounds fresh sour cherries, pitted, or 2 pounds frozen sour cherries, partially thawed

TO PREPARE THE PIECRUST

Roll out the pie dough into a round 14 inches wide and ¼ inch thick. Gently fit into a 10-inch pie plate. Fold the edges under and crimp. Refrigerate until firm, about 30 minutes.

TO MAKE THE PISTACHIO CRUMBLE

1. In a medium bowl, combine the all-purpose flour, oat flour, sugar, cinnamon, salt, and pistachios.
2. Stir in the melted butter and mix gently to combine.

BEFORE YOU MAKE THE FILLING

Place a rack in the bottom third of your oven. Preheat the oven to 350°F. Line a cookie sheet with parchment paper or aluminum foil.

TO MAKE THE CHERRY FILLING

1. In a small bowl, whisk together the sugar, cornstarch, and salt.
2. In a medium bowl, place the cherries and sprinkle the flour mixture over the top; mix gently to combine. (If you are using fresh cherries, the natural sweetness can vary. Taste the mixture to see if you need more sugar than is called for.)
3. Pour the cherries into the unbaked pie shell.

TO COMPLETE THE PIE

1. Sprinkle the pistachio crumble evenly over the top of the cherries.
2. Place the pie plate on the prepared cookie sheet. Bake for about 1 hour and 10 minutes, or until the juices are bubbling and thick. Remove to a rack to cool to room temperature before serving.

Fruit pies are best eaten the day they are baked.

PEAR CRANBERRY PIE WITH GINGERSNAP CRUMBLE

Pastry chefs know that pears can be a hard sell on a dessert menu. When I first created the pear cranberry pie for my Thanksgiving pie menu, I knew I'd have to add a delicious crumble topping to help create a following. This gingersnap crumble really did the trick. The following year, Food & Wine *featured it in its Thanksgiving issue, and it has beaten out pumpkin pie sales ever since. Go pears!*   **Makes one 9-inch pie**

FOR THE PIECRUST
½ recipe Flaky Pie Dough (page 137)

FOR THE GINGERSNAP CRUMBLE
1 cup all-purpose flour
¼ cup granulated sugar
¼ cup firmly packed light brown sugar
¼ pound Gingersnaps (page 64) (about 10 cookies), crushed
⅛ teaspoon ground ginger
½ teaspoon kosher salt
8 tablespoons (1 stick) unsalted butter, melted and cooled

FOR THE PEAR CRANBERRY FILLING
2 pounds ripe Bosc pears (about 6), peeled, cored, quartered,
  and cut into ¼-inch slices
1½ cups cranberries, fresh or frozen
1 teaspoon freshly grated lemon zest
2 tablespoons fresh lemon juice
½ teaspoon pure vanilla extract
½ cup granulated sugar
2 tablespoons cornstarch
¼ teaspoon salt

TO PREPARE THE PIECRUST

Roll the pie dough out into a round 12 inches wide and ¼ inch thick. Gently fit it into a 9-inch pie plate. Fold the edges under and crimp. Refrigerate until firm, about 30 minutes.

TO MAKE THE CRUMBLE

1. In a medium bowl, whisk together the flour, sugars, gingersnaps, ginger, and salt.

2. Stir in the melted butter.

You can make the crumble and store it in an airtight container at room temperature for up to 2 days, or in the refrigerator for up to 1 week. If refrigerating, be sure to let it come to room temperature for easier crumbling.

BEFORE YOU MAKE THE FILLING

Position a rack in the bottom third of your oven. Preheat the oven to 350°F. Line a cookie sheet with parchment paper or aluminum foil.

TO MAKE THE FILLING

1. In a medium bowl, combine the pears, cranberries, zest, lemon juice, and vanilla and mix gently.

2. In a small bowl, whisk together the sugar, cornstarch, and salt. Stir the sugar mixture into the fruit mixture.

3. Pour the fruit mixture into the unbaked pie shell.

TO COMPLETE THE PIE

1. Sprinkle the gingersnap crumble evenly over the top of the fruit mixture

2. Place the pie plate on the prepared cookie sheet. Bake for 1 hour and 15 minutes, or until the juices are bubbling and thick. Remove to a wire rack to cool to room temperature before serving.

Fresh fruit pies are best eaten the day they are baked.

NORTH FORK PEACH RASPBERRY PIE

My family used to have a weekend summer house on Shelter Island, just off the North Fork of Long Island. The car trip out there was grueling on those late Friday afternoons, for we were not the only family headed to the beach. The traffic was relentless. Once we exited the congested Long Island Expressway, we'd crawl through miles and miles of potato farms. The farm stand at Briermere Farm was our beacon as we neared the end of the road. We'd stop to stretch and pick up fresh vegetables and a couple of their home-made fruit pies. Their peach raspberry pie alone made the entire trip worthwhile. This recipe was inspired by that simple yet unforgettable tradition. **Makes one 10-inch pie**

FOR THE PIECRUST
1 recipe Flaky Pie Dough (page 137)

FOR PEACH RASPBERRY FILLING
¾ cup sugar plus 2 teaspoons, for sprinkling
2 tablespoons cornstarch
2 tablespoons tapioca pearls, ground to a flour
 (in a spice grinder)
⅛ teaspoon salt
6 cups peeled and sliced ripe peaches (about 3¼ pounds)
1 dry pint fresh raspberries
Finely grated zest of 1 lemon

FOR THE EGG WASH
1 large egg
2 tablespoons heavy cream
Pinch kosher salt

TO PREPARE THE PIECRUST

Roll out the pie dough into two rounds 14 inches wide and ¼ inch thick. Gently fit one into a 10-inch pie plate, and lay the other flat on a cookie sheet lined with parchment paper or aluminum foil. Cover with plastic wrap and refrigerate until ready to assemble, at least 30 minutes.

BEFORE YOU MAKE THE FILLING

Position a rack in the bottom third of your oven. Preheat the oven to 350°F. Line a cookie sheet with parchment paper or aluminum foil.

TO MAKE THE FILLING

1. In a small bowl, whisk together the sugar, cornstarch, tapioca flour, and salt.

2. In a large bowl, stir together the peaches, raspberries, and zest. Sprinkle the sugar mixture over the fruit and stir gently to combine.

3. Pour the fruit mixture into the unbaked pie shell.

4. Place the second dough layer over the filled pie shell. Fold under the edge and crimp.

TO COMPLETE THE PIE

1. *For the egg wash:* Using a fork, combine the egg with the heavy cream and salt.

2. Brush the top crust with the egg wash and sprinkle with the 2 teaspoons sugar. Cut 4 steam vents in the top crust.

3. Place pie plate on the prepared cookie sheet. Bake for 1 hour and 45 minutes, or until the juices are bubbling and thick. Remove to a wire rack to cool to room temperature before serving.

Fresh fruit pies are best eaten the day they are baked. This pie tastes great with freshly whipped cream (page 131).

This tart is very special, and so easy to make. I love the light custard that binds all of the cherries together. **Makes one 9-inch deep dish tart**

1 prebaked 9-inch tart shell made from Sweet Dough for Pies,
  Tarts, and Sugar Cookies (page 142)
⅔ **cup heavy cream**
⅔ **cup whole milk**
½ **vanilla bean**
3 **large eggs**
¼ **cup sugar**
1½ **tablespoons cornstarch**
Pinch kosher salt
¼ **teaspoon almond extract**
1 **cup frozen cherries, thawed and drained, or 1½ cups fresh**
  cherries, pitted
3 **tablespoons sliced blanched almonds, toasted, for sprinkling**
Confectioners' sugar, for sprinkling

BEFORE YOU START

Position a rack in the center of your oven. Preheat the oven to 350°F. Line a cookie sheet with parchment paper or aluminum foil.

FOR THE CUSTARD FILLING

1. In a heavy saucepan, stir together the heavy cream and the milk. Using a small paring knife, split the half vanilla bean and scrape out the seeds. Add the seeds and pod to the cream mixture. Place over medium heat and bring to scalding (see Note)— not boiling. Remove from the heat, cover, and set aside to steep for 10 minutes.

2. In a large bowl, whisk together the eggs, sugar, cornstarch, and salt. In a slow steady stream, whisk the still-warm cream mixture into the egg mixture. Stir in the almond extract. Strain the mixture through a fine-meshed strainer into a clean bowl.

3. Place the tart shell on the prepared cookie sheet. Scatter the cherries evenly over the bottom of the prebaked shell. Pour the custard over the cherries. Bake for 45 to 50 minutes, or until the custard is set. Remove to a wire rack to cool to room temperature.

4. Sprinkle the almonds around the edge of the tart and dust the almonds with confectioners' sugar.

Serve at room temperature or slightly chilled. This clafoutis is best eaten the day it is made.

Note: "Scalding" equals 180°F on a candy thermometer. Scalding liquid will be steaming, and tiny bubbles will form on the edges of the pan.

BEAR'S PEACH COBBLER

This is my little sister Erin's favorite dessert. The first time I made it was for her fifth birthday. It was the same year I gave her a little pumpkin-colored bunny that she named Candlelight. For her, that fifth birthday is hard to beat.

Makes one 2-quart cobbler (6 to 8 servings)

FOR THE COBBLER TOPPING
1 cup all-purpose flour
1 teaspoon baking powder
¼ teaspoon kosher salt
2 tablespoons sugar plus 1½ teaspoons, for sprinkling
½ teaspoon freshly grated lemon zest
2 tablespoons cold unsalted butter, cut into ¼-inch pieces
½ cup heavy cream
1 tablespoon whole milk or heavy cream, for glazing

FOR THE PEACH FILLING
6 cups peeled and sliced ripe, fresh peaches (about 3½ pounds)
Juice of 1 lemon
¾ cup sugar
2 tablespoons cornstarch
½ teaspoon ground cinnamon

1. In a large bowl, whisk together the flour, baking powder, salt, the 2 tablespoons sugar, and the zest. Using a pastry blender, cut in the butter until it resembles a coarse meal. Little by little stir in the heavy cream until the dough starts to hold together (a bit more cream may be used if need be).

2. Turn the dough out onto a lightly floured work surface. Pat together to form a round about ½ inch thick. Using a lightly floured 2½-inch round biscuit cutter, cut the dough into 7 or 8 biscuits.

3. Place the biscuits on a cookie sheet lined with parchment paper or aluminum foil and refrigerate, loosely covered with plastic wrap, until ready to use.

BEFORE YOU MAKE THE FILLING

Position a rack in the bottom third of your oven. Preheat the oven to 350°F. Butter a 2-quart ovenproof deep-dish pan. Line a cookie sheet with parchment paper or aluminum foil.

TO MAKE THE FILLING

1. In a medium bowl, stir together the peach slices, lemon juice, sugar, cornstarch, and cinnamon.

2. Pour the peach mixture into the prepared dish.

TO COMPLETE THE COBBLER

1. Place the biscuits evenly on top of the peach mixture. Brush with the milk. Sprinkle with the 1½ teaspoons sugar.

2. Place the dish on the prepared cookie sheet. Bake for 1 hour and 15 minutes. (To check the "doneness" of the biscuits, carefully lift one to see that the bottom looks like a steamed "dumpling" and not raw dough.) Remove to a wire rack to cool before serving.

This cobbler is best eaten the day it is baked. Serve warm with freshly whipped cream (page 131).

This double-crusted apple pie has a creamy caramel sauce that is mixed into the apples right before baking. The addition of lemon zest keeps the rich caramel in check.

Makes 1 cup sauce

FOR THE CARAMEL SAUCE
½ cup heavy cream
⅔ cup sugar
2 tablespoons water
3 tablespoons unsalted butter
¾ teaspoon pure vanilla extract

FOR THE PIECRUST
1 recipe Flaky Pie Dough (page 137) or All-Butter Pie Dough
 (page 140)

FOR THE APPLE FILLING
8 Granny Smith apples, peeled, cored, and cut into ½-inch slices
1 teaspoon freshly grated lemon zest
2 tablespoons all-purpose flour
3 tablespoons sugar
¼ teaspoon kosher salt
2 teaspoons sugar, for sprinkling

FOR THE EGG WASH
1 large egg
2 tablespoons heavy cream
Pinch kosher salt

TO MAKE THE SAUCE

1. In a small saucepan over medium heat, warm the heavy cream to hot but not boiling, 3 to 4 minutes.

2. In a medium heavy-bottomed saucepan over medium heat, combine the sugar, and water and heat until amber in color (like clover honey), about 10 minutes. Immedi-

ately remove the caramelized sugar from the heat. (Please be careful when caramelizing sugar—no kids in the room. Hot sugar is a very bad burn.)

3. Slowly pour the cream into the caramel, stirring with a wooden spoon. Stir in the butter and vanilla. Let cool to warm.

TO PREPARE THE PIECRUST

Roll out the dough into two rounds 14 inches wide and ¼ inch thick. Gently fit one into a 10-inch pie plate and lay the other flat on a cookie sheet lined with parchment paper or aluminum foil. Cover with plastic wrap and refrigerate until ready to assemble, at least 30 minutes.

BEFORE YOU MAKE THE FILLING

Position a rack in the bottom third of your oven. Preheat the oven to 350°F. Line a cookie sheet with parchment paper or aluminum foil.

TO MAKE THE FILLING

1. In a large bowl, stir together the apples, zest, flour, sugar, and salt to combine.
2. Stir the caramel sauce (which should be warm but not hot) into the apples.

TO COMPLETE THE PIE

1. *For the egg wash:* Whisk together the egg, heavy cream, and salt with a fork.
2. Pour the caramel apple filling into the unbaked pie shell. Brush the edges of the crust with some of the egg wash.
3. Place the second dough round on top of the filled pie shell. Fold under the edges and crimp.
4. Brush the top crust with the egg wash and sprinkle with the 2 teaspoons sugar. Cut 4 steam vents in the top crust.
5. Place the pie plate on the freshly lined cookie sheet. Bake for 1 hour and 45 minutes, or until the juices are bubbling and thick and the apples are tender. Remove to a wire rack to cool before serving.

This pie is best served warm or at room temperature. As with all fruit pies, it is best eaten the day it is baked.

LEMON BLUEBERRY BUTTERMILK PIE

Blueberries really need to be offset by something tart to taste their best. This pie is so delicious because the rich tang of buttermilk and fresh lemon juice shows off plump ripe blueberries. This one is really fun and easy to make.

Makes one 10-inch pie

FOR THE PIE
1 prebaked 10-inch piecrust made from All-Butter Pie Dough
  (page 140)
1½ cups sugar
1 tablespoon plus 1½ teaspoons cornstarch, sifted
8 tablespoons (1 stick) unsalted butter, melted
3 large eggs
1 teaspoon pure vanilla extract
½ cup buttermilk
2 teaspoons freshly grated lemon zest
2 tablespoons fresh lemon juice

FOR THE BLUEBERRY TOPPING
¼ cup apricot preserves
1 tablespoon water
1½ dry pints fresh blueberries, picked through,
  stems discarded

BEFORE YOU START

Position a rack in the center of your oven. Preheat the oven to 350°F. Line a cookie sheet with parchment paper or aluminum foil.

TO MAKE THE PIE

1. In a large bowl, whisk together the sugar, cornstarch, butter, eggs, vanilla, buttermilk, zest, and lemon juice until smooth.

2. Pour the buttermilk mixture into the prebaked pie shell.

3. Place the pie plate on the prepared cookie sheet. Bake for 40 minutes, or until the crust is golden brown and the custard is set. Remove to a wire rack to cool to room temperature before topping with the blueberries.

TO MAKE THE BLUEBERRY TOPPING

1. In a small heavy-bottomed saucepan over medium heat, whisk together the apricot preserves and the water until melted. Strain through a fine-meshed strainer into a medium bowl. Add the blueberries and, using a rubber spatula, stir gently to coat.

2. Pile the blueberries on top of the pie.

Serve the pie chilled or at room temperature. It keeps tightly wrapped in the refrigerator for up to 2 days.

APPLE ORCHARD PECAN CRUMBLE

Apple crumbles are one of the easiest desserts to put together. Just peel and slice the apples, mix the pecan crumble ingredients together and sprinkle them over the top, and pop the crumble in the oven. In about 20 minutes you'll start to smell it baking—and so will everyone in the house.

If you can, serve the Apple Orchard Pecan Crumble warm from the oven with some freshly whipped cream (page 131) or Brown Sugar Vanilla Ice Cream (page 184). You are guaranteed to get out of doing the dishes.

FOR THE APPLE ORCHARD FILLING
7 large tart apples (roughly 3 pounds), peeled, cored, and cut
 into ¼-inch slices (a combination of Macouns, McIntosh,
 Golden Delicious and Granny Smiths are great!)
Juice of 1 lemon
1 cup sugar
½ teaspoon ground cinnamon
1 tablespoon all-purpose flour

FOR THE PECAN CRUMBLE
¾ cup pecan pieces
¾ cup plus 2 tablespoons all-purpose flour
¾ cup firmly packed light brown sugar
¾ teaspoon salt
Pinch freshly grated nutmeg
⅛ teaspoon ground allspice
8 tablespoons (1 stick) unsalted butter, melted and cooled
 slightly

BEFORE YOU START

Position a rack in the bottom third of your oven. Preheat the oven to 350°F. Lightly butter a 10-inch deep-dish baking dish or 2-quart ovenproof casserole. Line a cookie sheet with parchment paper or aluminum foil.

TO MAKE THE FILLING

1. In a large bowl, stir together the apples and lemon juice. Sprinkle the sugar, cinnamon, and flour over the apples, and stir to combine.
2. Pour the apples into the baking dish.

TO MAKE THE CRUMBLE

1. In a large bowl, stir together the pecans, flour, brown sugar, salt, nutmeg, and allspice. Stir in the melted butter.

2. Spread the crumble over the apples.

TO COMPLETE THE CRUMBLE

Place the baking dish on the prepared cookie sheet. Bake for 1 hour and 20 minutes, or until the juices are bubbling and thick. Remove to a wire rack to cool before serving. Serve warm with whipped cream (page 131).

PRO TIP: Whether using fresh or dried fruits, crumbles are superconvenient because they may be assembled and frozen, and then baked whenever you wish. Simply preheat the oven, pull the dish from the freezer, loosely tent it with foil, and pop it in the oven. Pull off the foil about halfway through baking, and bake until the juices are bubbling and thick.

Fruit crumbles are best eaten the day they are baked, but they do keep better in the refrigerator than pies (no crust!). They can last up to 2 days. Wrap with plastic wrap or aluminum foil. Unwrap to warm in the oven or microwave for 30 seconds before serving.

PLUM RASPBERRY PIE WITH A SWEET ALMOND LATTICE

This almond lattice is special not only because it is beautiful to look at, but the sweet almond flavor is unexpected and delicious. Black plums make a pie with incredibly red juices. It's absolutely gorgeous.

Makes one 9-inch pie

FOR THE PIECRUST
½ recipe Flaky Pie Dough (page 137)

FOR THE ALMOND LATTICE
1 cup all-purpose flour
¼ cup sugar
⅛ teaspoon kosher salt
4 tablespoons (½ stick) cold unsalted butter,
  cut into ¼-inch pieces
3 tablespoons almond paste, broken into ½-inch pieces
1 large egg yolk
½ teaspoon pure vanilla extract
¼ teaspoon almond extract
2 tablespoons ice water

FOR THE EGG WASH
1 large egg
2 tablespoons heavy cream
Pinch kosher salt

FOR THE PLUM RASPBERRY FILLING
½ cup sugar
2 tablespoons cornstarch
2 tablespoons tapioca pearls, ground to a flour
  (use a spice grinder)
2¾ pounds black or red plums (about 8 large plums),
  washed, pitted, and cut into ½-inch slices
Finely grated zest from ½ orange
1 dry half pint fresh raspberries

TO PREPARE THE PIECRUST

Roll out the pie dough into a round 12 inches wide and ¼ inch thick (see Roll the Dough, page 138). Gently fit it into a 9-inch pie plate. Fold the edges under and crimp. Refrigerate until firm, about 30 minutes.

TO MAKE THE ALMOND LATTICE

1. In the bowl of a food processor fitted with the metal blade, pulse blend the flour, sugar, and salt to combine. Add the butter and almond paste and pulse until it is a coarse meal.

2. In a small bowl, whisk together the egg, vanilla, almond extract, and water with a fork. Add to the flour mixture and pulse until the dough looks uniformly moistened and crumbly.

3. Turn the dough out onto a lightly floured work suface. Pressing together with your hands, form the crumbly mixture into a disk measuring 6 inches in diameter. Loosely cover with plastic wrap and refrigerate for 20 minutes before rolling. For longer storage, wrap tightly in plastic wrap and refrigerate for up to 3 days, or freeze tightly wrapped in plastic wrap and then alumninum foil for up to 3 weeks.

4. When ready to roll, place a piece of parchment or wax paper on your work surface and, using a little flour, roll the dough into a round measuring 11 inches in diameter. Using a pizza wheel or chef's knife, cut strips measuring ¾ inch wide. Leave the lattice strips on the parchment, and transfer to a baking sheet. Wrap the lattice strips with plastic wrap and refrigerate until ready to assemble the pie, about 20 minutes.
   Preheat the oven to 350°F when you are ready to assemble the pie.

5. *For the egg wash:* Using a fork, whisk together the egg, heavy cream, and salt. Set aside.

BEFORE YOU MAKE THE FILLING

Position a rack in the bottom third of the oven. Preheat the oven to 350°F. Line a cookie sheet with parchment paper or aluminum foil.

TO MAKE THE FILLING

1. In a small bowl, whisk together the sugar, cornstarch, and tapioca flour.

2. In a large bowl, toss the plums and zest. Gently stir in the raspberries. Sprinkle the sugar mixture over the fruit and stir gently to combine.

3. Pour the filling into the unbaked pie shell.

TO COMPLETE THE PIE

1. Lay the lattice strips across the top of the pie in a crisscross pattern, pressing gently at the point where the lattice meets the rim of the crust to join them together.

2. Using a pastry brush, gently brush the egg wash over the crimped piecrust edges and the lattice.

3. Loosely cover the pie with aluminum foil. Bake for 30 minutes. Uncover the pie and bake for an additional 1 hour and 30 minutes, or until the fruit is bubbling and thick. Remove to a wire rack to cool to room temperature before serving.

Fresh fruit pies are best eaten the day they are baked.

MASTER RECIPE FOR PRESERVES

Making your own preserves is a lot of fun, and it can be quick and easy to do, especially if you are freezing them. Putting them up in jars is a little more time consuming, but still is not difficult.

I think the biggest mistake home cooks make when making preserves is taking on too much fruit! With a mountain of peaches to blanch, slice, cook, and can, preserving might become a chore and not at all fun. This recipe makes about a quart and easily multiplies for more. But don't go overboard! The whole process will be much more enjoyable if you limit yourself to ten pounds of fruit or less. As someone who has attempted to make way too much, trust me.

This is a great basic recipe. I use the Granny Smith apple as a natural source of pectin. You can play around with the ingredients as much as you like, but use this recipe as a guide, and increase it according to how much fruit you want to work with.

Makes about 1 quart

8 cups peeled and sliced ripe fresh fruit of your choice (2 dry quarts)

2 cups peeled and cubed Granny Smith apples (2 to 3 apples cut into ¼- to ½-inch pieces)

2 cups sugar

¼ cup fresh lemon and/or orange juice

2 tablespoons freshly grated citrus zest

1. In an 8-quart heavy-bottomed saucepan over medium heat, combine the fruit, apples, sugar, juice, and zest. Cook, until the mixture reaches 212°F on a candy thermometer, stirring often to prevent scorching. You may mash the fruit slightly with a potato masher, if necessary. Once the preserves have reached 212°F, continue to cook for 30 minutes more, stirring often, until thick. You can check the consistency by placing a dollop on a plate and setting it in the freezer until just cool. If it is runny, continue cooking; if it is thick, you're good to go.

2. Can the fruit in clean canning jars as directed by the manufacturer, or cool to room temperature, tightly cover, and refrigerate for up to 2 weeks, or freeze up to 6 months.

Cinnamon Peach

Peel and slice the peaches and add 3 cinnamon sticks to the fruit mixture. Use a combination of lemon and orange juice, but no zest.

Plum Raspberry Preserves

Use 1½ quarts unpeeled sliced plums and 2 cups raspberries. Use lemon juice and orange zest.

Strawberry Rhubarb Preserves with Fresh Orange

Use equal parts sliced rhubarb and hulled and sliced strawberries. Increase the sugar by ¾ cup. Use orange juice and orange zest.

Jumbleberry Preserves

Use a combination of raspberries, blueberries, blackberries, and strawberries; either lemon or orange juice; and either lemon zest or orange zest.

Strawberry–Ruby Grapefruit Preserves

Use 2 quarts strawberries, hulled and sliced, and the grated zest and juice of 2 ruby red grapefruits.

CHAPTER FIVE

SUNDAY SUPPER'S GRAND FINALE

Puddings, Specialty Pies, Cheesecakes,
and More

Pumpkin Bread Pudding with Caramel–Rum Raisin Sauce

Sweet Almond Bread Pudding with Raspberry Sauce

Easy Chocolate Mousse

Chocolate Pudding

Butterscotch Pudding

Perfect Pound Cake

Brown Sugar Vanilla Ice Cream

Sweet Melissa's Hot Fudge Sauce

Butterscotch Sauce

Pavlova Peach Melba

Lemon Blueberry Cheesecake with Cornmeal Crumble Crust

Coconut Custard Pie

Chocolate Bourbon Pecan Pie

Brown Butter Maple Pecan Pie

Chocolate Piecrust

Ginger Custard Pumpkin Pie

Chocolate Espresso Cheesecake with Blackberry Glaze

Speakeasy

Sacher Torte

Fallen Chocolate Soufflé Cake

Chocolate Raspberry Truffle Torte

Lemon Icebox Cake with Fresh Strawberry Sauce

IN OUR HOUSE, Sunday was "go outside and play" day. After church and our late-Sunday breakfast, we'd change into our play clothes and tear around on our bikes until supper was ready. We had a cow bell hanging from our back porch, right outside our kitchen, that my mom rang to call us in for dinner. No matter where we were in the neighborhood—at the dead end playing kickball or in the "mountains" playing army—we happily dropped what we were doing and came racing home. My mom did not have to ring twice. We'd all be home within five minutes. (I *was* late once: I was playing army with my big brothers and they captured me as their prisoner right away. When my mom rang the supper bell, I was left abandoned in the lap of a big tree (my jail cell) with *no* way to get down! Hours later (well, maybe minutes) Daddy *finally* sent them to fetch me.)

My mom often made dessert to end our supper, but she *always* made it on Sundays. Sometimes it would be butterscotch pudding (my dad's top choice) or a double-crusted apple pie, rich with ground cinnamon and cloves, that you could smell from the end of the driveway. We would be ravenous after playing all day and she'd have to make a big and hearty early supper, like chicken and dumplings or pot roast with gravy, carrots, and noodles. We always cleaned our plates and waited with anticipation for her to say, "Are you guys ready for dessert?" My mom knew exactly how to get her children to the dinner table.

PUMPKIN BREAD PUDDING
WITH CARAMEL–RUM RAISIN SAUCE

This is the one to serve if you want people to bow at your feet. It's totally unassuming, so you'll be able to say, "Oh, it's just a little bread pudding I threw together." But your guests are going to love it, even if they don't like caramel, rum, or raisins. It's super-crazy-yummy deliciousness.

Makes 8 to 10 servings bread pudding

FOR THE BREAD PUDDING
1 loaf brioche (about 1 pound)
2 cups whole milk
2 cups heavy cream
½ vanilla bean, split and scraped
3 cinnamon sticks, crushed
One 2-inch piece fresh ginger, coarsely chopped
6 whole cloves
5 large eggs
3 large egg yolks
¾ cup sugar
½ teaspoon kosher salt
1 cup pumpkin puree, fresh (see Note, page 197) or canned

FOR THE CINNAMON SUGAR
3 tablespoons sugar
½ teaspoon cinnamon

FOR THE CARAMEL–RUM RAISIN SAUCE
¼ cup dark rum
⅓ cup raisins
1 cup sugar
3 tablespoons water
¾ cup heavy cream

Position a rack in the center of your oven. Preheat the oven to 325°F. Lightly butter a 2-quart baking dish.

TO MAKE THE BREAD PUDDING

1. Cut the brioche into 1-inch pieces. Lay them on a cookie sheet in an even layer and lightly toast them in the oven to dry, about 10 minutes.

2. In a medium saucepan over medium heat, combine the milk, heavy cream, vanilla bean pod and seeds, cinnamon sticks, ginger, and cloves and heat to scalding, or until the cream is steaming and tiny bubbles have formed along the edges. Do not boil. Remove from the heat and cover with aluminum foil. Let steep for at least 20 minutes.

3. In a large bowl, whisk together the eggs, egg yolks, sugar, salt, and pumpkin puree until very smooth.

4. When the cream mixture has steeped, reheat the cream over medium heat until hot but not boiling. Temper the cream mixture into the egg mixture, pouring it little by little and whisking all the while.

5. Place the toasted brioche in the prepared pan. Strain the custard over the bread and press down lightly with your hands so that all bread is soaking. Let soak for 20 minutes.

6. *For the cinnamon sugar:* In a small bowl, combine the sugar and cinnamon. Sprinkle on top of the bread pudding.

7. Place the baking dish inside a roasting pan large enough to hold it. Fill the roasting pan with hot water until it reaches halfway up the sides of the baking dish. Bake for 1 hour and 15 minutes, or until set. It will poof slightly when ready. Remove to a wire rack to cool to warm before serving.

TO MAKE THE SAUCE

1. In a microwave on high, heat the rum and raisins for 30 seconds.

2. In a small saucepan, heat the cream to scalding; do not boil.

3. In a medium saucepan over high heat, combine the sugar and water and heat until amber in color (like clover honey). (Please be careful when caramelizing sugar—no

kids in the room. Hot sugar is a very bad burn.) Remove from the heat and quickly stir in a little of the hot heavy cream to stop the cooking. Add the remaining heavy cream, stirring until smooth, and then stir in the rum and raisins.

Serve warm from the baking dish with the caramel–rum raisin sauce. The bread pudding keeps tightly wrapped in plastic wrap in the refrigerator for up to 3 days. Warm before serving. The sauce will keep in an airtight container in the refrigerator for up to 1 week. Warm and stir before serving.

PRO TIP: When making bread puddings, dry bread is best. The less moisture or water that is present in the loaf, the more room there is for the custard to soak into. This results in a bread pudding that is creamy and custardy, not soggy.

SWEET ALMOND BREAD PUDDING WITH RASPBERRY SAUCE

This bread pudding is one of our most popular desserts at Sweet Melissa Pâtisserie. I thought it would be too simple for my customers! You must *serve it with the raspberry sauce. The sauce takes it to another level.* **Makes 8 to 10 servings bread pudding**

1 stale brioche (about 1 pound), cut into 1-inch pieces
1 quart heavy cream
¾ cup sugar
6 large egg yolks
1 teaspoon pure vanilla extract
1 teaspoon almond extract
1½ teaspoons sugar
¼ cup sliced blanched almonds
1 recipe Raspberry Sauce (page 176)

BEFORE YOU START

Position a rack in the center of your oven. Preheat the oven to 325°F. Lightly butter a 2-quart baking dish.

1. Cut the brioche into 1-inch pieces. Lay them on a cookie sheet in an even layer and lightly toast them in the oven to dry, about 10 minutes.

2. In a medium saucepan over medium heat, combine the heavy cream with about half of the sugar, and heat to scalding, or until the cream is steaming and tiny bubbles have formed along the edges. Do not boil.

3. In a large bowl, whisk together the egg yolks and the rest of the sugar until smooth.

4. Temper the cream mixture into the egg yolks, pouring it little by little and whisking all the while. Stir in the vanilla and almond extract. Set aside and keep warm.

5. Place the toasted brioche in the prepared pan. Strain the custard over the bread and press down lightly with your hands so that all the bread is soaking. Let soak for 20 minutes.

6. Sprinkle the top of the bread pudding with the sugar and almonds.

7. Place the baking dish inside a roasting pan large enough to hold it. Fill the roasting pan with hot water until it reaches halfway up the sides of the baking dish. Bake for 1 hour and 15 minutes, or until set. It will poof slightly when ready. Remove to a wire rack to cool to warm before serving.

Serve warm from the baking dish with the cold raspberry sauce. The bread pudding keeps tightly wrapped in plastic wrap in the refrigerator for up to 3 days. Warm before serving.

PRO TIP: When making bread puddings, dry bread is best. The less moisture or water that is present in the loaf, the more room there is for the custard to soak into. This results in a bread pudding that is creamy and custardy, not soggy.

RASPBERRY SAUCE

Makes 2 cups sauce

**Two 12-ounce packages frozen unsweetened raspberries,
thawed, or 2½ dry pints fresh
¾ cup plus 2 tablespoons sugar
1 tablespoon fresh lemon juice**

1. In a medium saucepan over medium heat, stir together the raspberries, sugar, and lemon juice until it comes to a simmer. Simmer for 2 minutes. Remove from the heat and let cool briefly.

2. In a food processor fitted with the metal blade or a blender, pulse the raspberry mixture until smooth. Strain the mixture into a resealable container and refrigerate for 2 hours.

Raspberry sauce will keep refrigerated in an airtight container for up to 5 days, or frozen for up to 1 month. Shake well before serving.

NOT SO PRO TIP: Wanna cheat? Don't feel like making raspberry sauce? Pick up an all-natural raspberry sorbet from the freezer section at your supermarket or grocery store. All you'll have to do is let it melt for a great and easy raspberry sauce!

EASY CHOCOLATE MOUSSE

Your friends will be really impressed if you serve this after dinner. Don't tell them how easy it is. Let them be impressed.
Makes 6 servings

5½ ounces best-quality semisweet (58%) chocolate, coarsely
  chopped
3 large egg whites at room temperature
¼ cup sugar
1⅔ cups cold heavy cream
1 teaspoon pure vanilla extract
2 tablespoons confectioners' sugar

1. In the top of a double boiler set over simmering, not boiling, water, melt the chocolate, stirring occasionally. Remove from the double boiler and set aside to cool to room temperature.

2. In the bowl of an electric mixer set over a pot of simmering, not boiling, water, whisk the egg whites with the sugar until the sugar has dissolved (feel with your fingers for sugar grains at the bottom of your bowl). Transfer the bowl to the electric mixer fitted with the whip attachment, and whip until the peaks are stiff but not dry.

3. Add one-quarter of this meringue to the cooled chocolate and whisk to blend. Gently fold in the remainder of the meringue until mostly incorporated (it can be slightly streaky at this point).

4. In the clean bowl of the electric mixer, whip the cream, vanilla, and confectioners' sugar to medium-soft peaks. Gently fold the whipped cream into the chocolate meringue mixture until just incorporated.

5. Transfer the mousse to a serving bowl, or pipe it into individual bowls. Cover the bowl(s) with plastic wrap and refrigerate for 1 hour, or until set.

Serve chilled, garnished with fresh berries, if desired. The mousse may be kept in an airtight container in the refrigerator for 2 days, or frozen for up to 3 weeks.

CHOCOLATE PUDDING

I used to make this when I worked at Home restaurant, in the West Village of Manhattan, around 1996. Home became famous for this chocolate pudding. It was so thick and creamy on your tongue, one of the richest desserts I have ever eaten—and one of the best.

Makes 6 servings pudding

3 cups heavy cream
¼ cup plus 1 tablespoon sugar
2¼ ounces best-quality semisweet (58%) chocolate,
  finely chopped (about ½ cup)
5 large egg yolks
½ teaspoon salt
¼ teaspoon pure vanilla extract

BEFORE YOU START

Position a rack in the center of your oven. Preheat the oven to 300°F. Place six 6-ounce ramekins in a 9 x 13-inch roasting pan.

1. In a medium, heavy-bottomed saucepan, bring the cream and about half of the sugar to scalding, or until the milk is steaming and tiny bubbles have formed along the edges. Do not boil.

2. Place the chopped chocolate in a medium-size bowl. Pour enough scalding cream over the chocolate to cover. Let sit for 5 minutes and then whisk until smooth. Pour the remaining cream over the chocolate and whisk until smooth.

3. In a large bowl, gently whisk together the egg yolks, the remaining half of the sugar, the salt, and vanilla until smooth. Temper the chocolate cream into the yolk mixture, pouring it little by little and whisking all the while. Strain the mixture into a clean pitcher and skim off any bubbles with a spoon.

4. Pour the mixture into the prepared ramekins. Fill the roasting pan with hot water until it reaches halfway up the sides of the ramekins. Cover the pan with aluminum foil. Bake for 50 to 60 minutes, or until just set. Begin checking after 45 minutes. When gently shaken, a pudding should no longer look liquidy; it

will move as one mass (albeit somewhat jiggly) and register 150° to 155°F on an instant-read thermometer. Remove to a wire rack to cool to room temperature in the water bath. Remove the ramekins from the pan and refrigerate, uncovered, until cool. Cover with plastic wrap and chill for several hours to overnight before serving.

BUTTERSCOTCH PUDDING

When Home's chef/owner David Page opened a sister restaurant, Drover's Tap Room, he asked me, his pastry chef at the time, to develop a butterscotch pudding to call Drover's own. Not so easy! The recipe needed to be free of cornstarch—just like the Chocolate Pudding (page 178) at Home—using only egg yolks as a thickener. After a month of testing and endless tastings, David put yet another spoonful of hopeful butterscotch pudding in his mouth. "That's it," he said, and left the room.

There is really only one trick to this pudding, and that is caramelizing the sugar. The goal is to get the sugar to be the color of amber—too dark and the pudding will taste bitter and burned. You may burn the sugar the first time, but you'll quickly get the hang of it. When you do try to caramelize the sugar, if the sugar smells burned or starts smoking, stop what you're doing, carefully add a little water to stop the scorching, put the pan in the sink and let it soak. Then start again! There is no turning back when you burn the sugar. Luckily, sugar is the least expensive of all the ingredients. (Note: Please be careful when caramelizing sugar—no kids in the room! Hot sugar is a very bad burn.)

Makes 6 servings pudding

6 large egg yolks
¼ cup firmly packed dark brown sugar
1 cup whole milk
2 cups heavy cream
½ cup granulated sugar
¼ cup water
1 teaspoon fine table salt
1 teaspoon pure vanilla extract

BEFORE YOU START

Position a rack in the center of your oven. Preheat the oven to 300°F. Place six 6-ounce ramekins in a 9 x 13-inch roasting pan.

1. In a large bowl, lightly whisk the egg yolks until smooth.

2. In a medium heavy-bottomed saucepan over medium-high heat, combine the brown sugar, milk, and heavy cream and heat to scalding, or until the milk is steaming and

tiny bubbles have formed along the edges. Do not boil. Stir frequently to dissolve the brown sugar. Remove from the heat.

3. While the cream mixture is heating, in a medium heavy-bottomed saucepan over low heat, stir together the granulated sugar and water. Increase the heat to high and boil the sugar. When the sugar starts to sputter, use a pastry brush dipped in water to wash down the sides of the pan. As soon as the sugar turns amber in color (like clover honey), remove from the heat and slowly and carefully pour in the hot cream while stirring to stop the cooking. (The caramel will bubble as you add the cream, so use a long wooden spoon or whisk to stir them.)

4. In a slow, steady stream, slowly and gently whisk the hot caramel mixture into the egg yolks. Stir in the salt and vanilla. Strain the mixture into a clean pitcher and skim off any air bubbles with a spoon.

5. Pour the mixture into the prepared ramekins. Fill the roasting pan with hot water until it reaches halfway up the sides of the ramekins. Cover the pan with aluminum foil. Bake for 50 to 60 minutes, or until just set. Begin checking after 45 minutes. When gently shaken, a pudding should no longer look liquidy; it will move as one mass (albeit somewhat jiggly) and register 150° to 155°F on an instant-read thermometer. Remove to a wire rack to cool to room temperature in the water bath.

6. Remove the ramekins from the pan. Refrigerate for several hours until chilled. Serve. For longer storage, once chilled, wrap each individually with plastic wrap and refrigerate.

Serve chilled with freshly whipped cream (page 131). The puddings keep covered with plastic wrap in the refrigerator for up to 5 days.

PERFECT POUND CAKE

It was a Thursday at Sweet Melissa's, the day we'd make the loaf cakes for our customers to have for the weekend. Jessie, my pastry sous-chef, had asked me the day before, "What kind of loaf cakes do you want to make tomorrow?" I didn't know. I'd grown tired of the ones I'd made over the previous month, too much going on—berries, zest, juice, poppy seeds, glaze, nuts. I wasn't in the mood for any of it.

I went to my books for inspiration. Chocolate chips, streusel, pecans. I was being assaulted by add-ins. I closed my eyes and thought, "What do I want to eat?" I realized I wanted gentle texture, supported by butter, vanilla, and a little salt. What I wanted was the perfect pound cake.

Now this was an important mission. How could I have come as far as I had without the perfect pound cake? I was dumbfounded by my own shortcoming. Sure, I had made lots of pound cakes, as the base for this and that, or as the body of a raspberry lemon loaf, but had I made the perfect pound cake? I had not. It was time I did.

I played around with some recipes: Some used all butter, some added heavy cream. I fooled with the temperature of the butter, trying both softened and melted, and ultimately found myself in front of the most gorgeous batter I had ever seen. "I could swim in this batter," I told Jessie. "It is nice. . . ," she replied without commitment. She had seen me testing recipes before, seen me excited about a batter, and even dealt with me sticking a batter-covered finger into her mouth from time to time.

"Jessie, you know that crack that pound cake has, where the center can get a little moist and yummy? That's my favorite part."

She said, with noticeable doubt in her voice, as if preparing me for the possible impossibility, "You may be asking too much,"

"Well, let's see." And I put the loaf into the oven.

Makes 1 pound cake

3 large eggs, at room temperature
1 cup sugar
¼ teaspoon kosher salt
1¾ cups cake flour
½ teaspoon baking powder
2½ teaspoons pure vanilla extract
½ cup heavy cream, at room temperature
6 tablespoons unsalted butter, melted
  and then cooled to warm

BEFORE YOU START

Position a rack in the center of your oven. Preheat the oven to 350°F. Lightly butter and flour a 1½-quart loaf pan.

1. In a large bowl, whisk together the eggs, sugar, and salt until smooth.

2. In a medium bowl, whisk together the cake flour and baking powder until evenly combined.

3. In a small bowl, stir together the vanilla and heavy cream to combine.

4. Sift one-third of the flour mixture over the egg mixture and whisk together until mostly incorporated. Pour half of the cream mixture over and whisk until mostly combined. Repeat with one-third more of the flour, followed by the remaining half of the cream mixture and the remaining flour. Do not overmix!

5. Pour the melted butter over the batter and fold in gently until incorporated. The batter will be silky and gorgeous.

6. Pour the batter into the prepared loaf pan. Bake for 50 minutes, or until a wooden skewer inserted into the center comes out clean. Remove to a wire rack to cool for 20 minutes before turning out the cake onto the rack.

ULTIMATE INDULGENCE: Try this the next time you have a cookout: Lightly grill several slices of pound cake and some fresh pineapple sliced about ¾ inch thick. Top the pound cake with some vanilla ice cream, the grilled pineapple, and a healthy drizzle of Butterscotch Sauce (page 186). I'm telling you, we could take over the world with this stuff.

The pound cake keeps well wrapped in plastic wrap at room temperature for 2 days. For longer storage, refrigerate tightly wrapped in plastic wrap for up to 5 days, or freeze wrapped in plastic wrap and then aluminum foil for up to 1 month. Do not unwrap before defrosting.

BROWN SUGAR VANILLA ICE CREAM

The secret to this ice cream's luxurious texture is the skim milk powder, an ingredient found in the supermarket that we don't often work with. The dry milk absorbs a lot of the water in the heavy cream and milk. The brown sugar adds to the richness, and the two different forms of vanilla create depth. You will need an ice cream maker for this recipe.
Makes 1 quart ice cream

2 cups heavy cream
1 cup skim milk
½ cup firmly packed light brown sugar
⅛ teaspoon salt
¼ cup dry skim milk powder
5 large egg yolks
½ vanilla bean, split and scraped, reserving the seeds and pod
½ teaspoon pure vanilla extract

1. Fill a large pot with about 3 inches of water and bring to a simmer. Set a large bowl over the top, and check that the bottom of the bowl does not touch the water (this is a double broiler or bain-marie setup). (Remove the bowl and use it to combine the ingredients for the ice cream.)

2. In the large bowl, whisk together the heavy cream, milk, brown sugar, salt, skim milk powder, egg yolks, vanilla bean and seeds, and vanilla until completely combined.

3. Place the bowl on top of the simmering pot. Be sure the water is simmering, not boiling. Cook, stirring constantly, until the mixture has thickened to *nappante* (thick enough to coat the back of the spoon), 5 to 10 minutes or approximately 180° to 185°F on a candy thermometer.

4. Cool the custard in an ice bath (see Note, page 99). Strain the mixture into a resealable container. Refrigerate for 4 hours or overnight.

5. Pour into an ice cream maker and freeze according to the manufacturer's instructions.

6. Transfer to a resealable container and freeze 4 hours or overnight before serving.

Try topping this ice cream with hot fudge (page 185) when you are ready to serve! The ice cream keeps frozen in an airtight container for up to 3 weeks.

SWEET MELISSA'S HOT FUDGE SAUCE

This hot fudge is the best I've ever eaten. It is sophisticated, not too sweet, and is amazing poured over Brown Sugar Vanilla Ice Cream (page 184) and topped with peanut praline (page 227). Use the best-quality chocolate and cocoa powder you can get your hands on. They are what make the difference. **Makes 1 quart sauce**

15 ounces best-quality bittersweet (64 to 68%) chocolate,
 coarsely chopped
½ cup sugar
1 cup plus 1 teaspoon light corn syrup
1 cup plus 2 teaspoons water
1½ cups unsweetened Dutch-process cocoa powder
1½ teaspoons instant coffee or instant espresso powder
2 tablespoons cognac or brandy

1. In the top of a double boiler set over simmering, not boiling, water, melt the chocolate, stirring occasionally. Keep warm.

2. In a large nonreactive saucepan over medium heat, combine sugar, corn syrup, water, cocoa powder, and instant coffee. Bring to a boil, whisking constantly. When the mixture comes to a rolling boil, cook for 1 to 2 more minutes.

3. Remove from the heat and whisk in the melted chocolate. Stir in the cognac.

Great served warm with Fallen Chocolate Soufflé Cake (page 204), or over Brown Sugar Vanilla Ice Cream (page 184) and Chocolate Walnut Brownies (page 82), or over the Brown Sugar Ice Cream and Peanut Brittle Praline. The sauce can be kept in an airtight container in the refrigerator for up to 3 weeks. Warm before serving in the microwave on medium high in 30-second intervals, stirring after each one.

BUTTERSCOTCH SAUCE

Any excuse to eat butterscotch sauce is a good one. Pouring butterscotch over Brown Sugar Vanilla Ice Cream (page 184) and bananas and then sprinkling it with coarsely chopped salted almonds is a little more civilized than just eating the sauce straight by the spoonful.

Makes 3 cups sauce

8 tablespoons (1 stick) unsalted butter
⅔ cup firmly packed dark brown sugar
⅔ cup granulated sugar
1½ teaspoons kosher salt
2 tablespoons water
¾ cup light corn syrup
¾ cup heavy cream
2 teaspoons pure vanilla extract

1. In a medium heavy-bottomed saucepan over medium heat, melt the butter. Stir in the brown sugar, granulated sugar, salt, water, and corn syrup and heat until the mixture comes to a boil. Boil for 3 minutes.

2. Remove from the heat and whisk in the heavy cream and vanilla until smooth.

3. Return the pan to the stove and, over low heat, simmer for 2 minutes. Allow to cool to warm.

Serve warm or at room temperature. This sauce can be kept tightly covered in the refrigerator for up to 2 weeks. Before serving, warm the sauce over low heat while whisking.

ULTIMATE INDULGENCE: For a heavenly sundae, serve the sauce over Brown Sugar Vanilla Ice Cream (page 184) and top it with a handful of chopped roasted salted almonds.

PAVLOVA PEACH MELBA

This is a really lovely dessert. It is gorgeous, and so light you can eat at least two servings. (And trust me, you'll want to!) Be sure your egg whites are very fresh, so the Pavlova will look like a puffy cloud. A Pavlova is lighter than air, just like the great Russian ballerina Anna Pavlova, its namesake. The fluffy meringue cloud will indeed remind you of the dancers' tutu.

Makes 8 servings

FOR THE MERINGUE
4 large egg whites
1 cup superfine sugar (see Note)
1½ teaspoons cornstarch
1 teaspoon white vinegar
¼ teaspoon pure vanilla extract

FOR THE MELBA
2 to 3 large ripe peaches, rinsed
1 pint fresh raspberries
1 recipe Raspberry Sauce (page 176)

FOR THE WHIPPED CREAM
1 cup cold heavy cream
1 teaspoon pure vanilla extract
1 tablespoon sugar

BEFORE YOU START

Position a rack in the center of your oven. Preheat the oven to 250°F. Line a baking sheet with parchment paper. Draw a 7-inch circle on the paper with a pen. Flip over the paper. (You should still be able to see the circle.)

TO MAKE THE MERINGUE

1. In a clean, grease-free bowl of an electric mixer fitted with the whip attachment, beat the egg whites on medium-high speed until they hold firm peaks, about 1 minute. Start adding the sugar, little by little, until the meringue holds very stiff glossy peaks, about 2 minutes. (You should not feel any sugar grains at this point. If you do, keep beating.)

2. Remove the bowl from the mixer. Sift the cornstarch over the meringue, and sprinkle the vinegar and vanilla on top. Using a rubber spatula, gently fold the ingredients into the meringue until just fully incorporated (the goal is to do so without deflating the meringue).

3. Gently mound the meringue in the center of the circle on the prepared parchment, and smooth the edges. Bake for 1 hour and 25 minutes. Turn off the oven, and allow the meringue to cool completely in the oven for an additional hour or more. The meringue may crack as it cools—this is normal. When cool, carefully peel the paper from the bottom of the meringue and place the meringue on a serving platter. The meringue can be made only the day of serving.

TO PREPARE THE FRUIT

Peel, pit, and slice the peaches and place them in a large bowl. Place the raspberries on top of the peaches. Pour over ½ cup raspberry sauce. Using a rubber spatula, gently combine. Set aside.

TO MAKE THE WHIPPED CREAM

In the bowl of an electric mixer fitted with the whip attachment, beat the heavy cream and vanilla on medium speed. In a slow steady stream, add the sugar beating until the mixture forms medium-stiff peaks.

TO COMPLETE THE PAVLOVA

1. Mound the whipped cream in the center of the meringue and spread it just up to the edges.

2. Pile the fruit and any sauce left in the bottom of the bowl on top of the cream.

3. Drizzle a little of the remaining raspberry sauce over the fruit, and serve the rest of the sauce on the side. Using a large spoon, serve immediately.

The Pavlova is best eaten the day it is made.

Note: You can make superfine sugar by blending granulated sugar in a food processor for 20 seconds.

NOT SO PRO TIP: If you want to make things really easy, instead of making raspberry sauce, you can buy an all-natural raspberry sorbet and let it melt. Instant sauce!

LEMON BLUEBERRY CHEESECAKE
WITH CORNMEAL CRUMBLE CRUST

I love creating flavored cheesecakes with all different types of interesting crusts. The coarse yellow cornmeal in this crust stays crunchy, and is just so delicious.

Makes one 9-inch cheesecake (12 servings)

FOR THE CORNMEAL CRUMBLE CRUST
8 tablespoons (1 stick) unsalted butter, softened
5 tablespoons sugar
½ cup all-purpose flour
½ cup coarse yellow cornmeal
Pinch fine salt

FOR THE LEMON CHEESECAKE
2 pounds (four 8-ounce packages) cream cheese, softened
1 cup mascarpone cheese
1½ cups sugar
2 large eggs
2 teaspoons finely grated lemon zest
3 tablespoons fresh lemon juice

FOR THE BLUEBERRY TOPPING
1 dry pint fresh blueberries, rinsed
½ cup sugar
1 tablespoon water
2 teaspoons fresh lemon juice

BEFORE YOU START

Position a rack in the center of your oven. Preheat the oven to 350°F. Turn a 9-inch springform pan upside down and cover the bottom and sides with aluminum foil. The foil should come up at least halfway on all sides, so that the water from the water bath will not leak through. Line the bottom of the springform pan with parchment cut to fit exactly. Using a nonstick vegetable cooking spray, spray the inside papered bottom and sides of the pan.

TO MAKE THE CRUST

1. In the bowl of an electric mixer fitted with the paddle attachment, cream together the butter and sugar, 1 to 1½ minutes. Add the flour, cornmeal, and salt and mix until combined.

2. Press the mixture onto the bottom and up the sides of the springform pan. (I use a cup with a flat base to help me press the crumbs evenly up the sides.) Bake for about 25 to 30 minutes, or until golden. Remove to a wire rack to cool. Lower the oven to 325°F.

TO MAKE THE CHEESECAKE MIXTURE

1. In the bowl of an electric mixer fitted with the paddle attachment, cream together the cream cheese, mascarpone, and sugar until smooth. Scrape down the bowl and the paddle. Add the eggs and mix to combine. Add the lemon zest and lemon juice.

2. Pour the batter into the prepared crust and spin gently to level the batter.

3. Place the springform pan in a roasting pan large enough to hold it. Fill the roasting pan with hot water until it reaches halfway up the sides of the springform pan. Bake for about 1 hour and 30 minutes, or until the center is just set. Remove the pan from the water bath and remove the aluminum foil on top. Using a sharp knife, loosen the edges of the cheesecake from the pan. Let cool on a wire rack to room temperature. Remove the bottom foil liner and refrigerate until chilled, at least 4 hours to overnight.

TO MAKE THE BLUEBERRY TOPPING

1. In a medium saucepan over low heat, combine half of the blueberries, the sugar, water, and lemon juice and cook until thick, 5 to 10 minutes.

2. Remove from the heat and stir in the remaining blueberries. Let cool to room temperature or refrigerate for about 30 minutes.

TO COMPLETE THE CHEESACAKE

1. Once the cheesecake is chilled, release the springform ring from around it. To remove the bottom, slide two offset spatulas under the cake and transfer it to a serving plate.

2. Spoon the topping over the cheesecake and serve.

The topped cheesecake will keep in a cake saver in the refrigerator for up to 3 days. If you want to, you can make the cheesecake and the blueberry sauce ahead. Store them tightly wrapped separately for up to 3 days. Top the cheesecake before serving.

COCONUT CUSTARD PIE

When I was growing up, coconut custard was my dad's favorite pie. It wasn't my favorite back then: I disliked the texture of the coconut. Well, now I'm a big fan, and while updating my Thanksgiving pie menu for Sweet Melissa's, I realized this is what I'd been missing. Initially, I added too much coconut to the filling, figuring the more the better! (Yeah, these days I'm a really big coconut fan.) But then I realized that with too much coconut, the silkiness of the custard gets lost. Well, this recipe is just right.

Makes one 9-inch pie

FOR THE PIECRUST
**1 prebaked 9-inch pie shell made from
 All-Butter Pie Dough (page 140)**

FOR THE COCONUT CUSTARD FILLING
3 large eggs
½ cup sugar
⅔ teaspoon cornstarch
¼ teaspoon kosher salt
1 cup heavy cream
⅔ cup whole milk
1 tablespoon pure vanilla extract
Pinch ground cinnamon
Pinch freshly ground nutmeg
1 cup sweetened coconut
1½ tablespoons unsalted butter at room temperature

BEFORE YOU START

Position a rack in the bottom third of your oven. Preheat the oven to 325°F.

FOR THE FILLING

1. In a blender, pulse the eggs until pale yellow, about 15 seconds. Add the sugar, cornstarch, and salt. Pulse to combine, about 15 seconds more. Add the heavy cream, milk, vanilla, cinnamon, and nutmeg. Pulse blend for 30 seconds more.

2. Sprinkle the coconut evenly over the bottom of the prebaked pie shell. Pour in the custard. Dot the top of the pie with small pieces of the butter. Bake for 50 to 55 minutes, or until golden and set. Remove to a wire rack to cool.

I like to eat this pie when it has just cooled to warm, but it keeps tightly wrapped in plastic wrap in the refrigerator for up to 3 days (the crust will suffer slightly).

CHOCOLATE BOURBON PECAN PIE

I had a problem with the underrepresentation of chocolate at our Thanksgiving table, so I was determined to get some of it into one of my pies. This chocolate bourbon pecan pie is just right. The crust is not too sweet, but rich with dark cocoa. The filling is made with pure maple syrup, browned butter, and bourbon, and the dark chocolate just melts into the pecans. This is a winner and will forever remain on Sweet Melissa's Thanksgiving pie menu. (Try it with a scoop of coffee ice cream—wow!)

Makes one 9-inch pie

FOR THE PIE CRUST
1 prebaked 9-inch Chocolate Piecrust (page 195)

FOR THE CHOCOLATE BOURBON PECAN FILLING
4 tablespoons (½ stick) unsalted butter
3 large eggs
½ cup sugar
6 tablespoons pure maple syrup
6 tablespoons dark corn syrup
1 tablespoon bourbon
¼ cup best-quality semisweet (58%) chocolate chips
1 cup shelled pecan pieces

BEFORE YOU START

Position a rack in the center of your oven. Preheat the oven to 350°F. Line a cookie sheet with parchment paper or aluminum foil.

FOR THE FILLING

1. In a small heavy-bottomed saucepan over medium heat, melt the butter until the milk solids turn golden brown. Immediately remove from heat and set aside to cool.

2. In a large bowl, using a whisk or hand blender, combine the eggs and sugar. Whisk in the maple syrup and dark corn syrup, and then the browned butter. Whisk in the bourbon.

3. Place the prebaked piecrust on the prepared cookie sheet. Sprinkle the chocolate chips and pecan pieces evenly over the bottom of the piecrust. Pour the bourbon mixture into the piecrust.

4. Bake for 40 to 45 minutes, or until the filling is set. Remove to a wire rack to cool to room temperature.

Serve slightly warm or at room temperature with freshly whipped cream (page 131) or Brown Sugar Vanilla Ice Cream (page 184). The pie keeps well wrapped in plastic wrap at room temperature for 2 days, or in the refrigerator for up to 4 days (the crust will suffer slightly if chilled).

Brown Butter Maple Pecan Pie

Simply start with a prebaked 9-inch pie shell made with All-Butter Pie Dough (page 140) or Flaky Pie Dough (page 137). Omit the chocolate chips. This is great when served with a scoop of vanilla or coffee ice cream.

CHOCOLATE PIECRUST

One 9- or 10-inch bottom crust

1 cup plus 2 teaspoons all-purpose flour
⅓ cup best-quality unsweetened Dutch-process cocoa powder
2 tablespoons sugar
½ teaspoon kosher salt
2 tablespoons cold unsalted butter, cut into ¼-inch pieces
¼ cup cold solid vegetable shortening
3 to 4 tablespoons ice water

1. In a large bowl, whisk together the flour, cocoa powder, sugar, and salt. Toss the cold butter into the flour mixture. Using a pastry blender, cut the butter into the flour until it is the size of large peas.

2. Pinch off small pieces of the shortening into the flour mixture and toss to coat. Using the pastry blender, continue cutting the butter and the shortening into the flour mixture, until they are the size of small peas.

3. Make a well in the center of the flour mixture. Pour about half of the water into the well, and, with a fork, pull the flour into the well. Continue mixing until the dough just comes together. Add more water, if needed.

4. Turn the dough out onto a lightly floured work surface. Gather the dough into a ball. Flatten it into a round disk, wrap it in plastic wrap, and refrigerate for at least 1 hour before rolling it out.

5. Roll out the dough to fit into the 9-inch or 10-inch pie plate. Fold the edges under and crimp. Prebake as directed (see page 139). (See pages 133–36 for instructions on rolling, crimping, and prebaking pie dough. Be sure to adjust these instructions for a 9-inch or 10-inch crust.)

The dough keeps tightly wrapped in plastic wrap in the refrigerator for up to 4 days, and frozen for up to 3 weeks. Do not unwrap before thawing.

I was born on Thanksgiving, so it is an extra-special holiday to me. My mom always tells me that she gives thanks for having me on this day. When my family hosted Thanksgiving dinner as I was growing up, the day always started out with special preparations for the afternoon's big feast. I would tend to the important dishes and stuff celery stalks with cream cheese and walnuts, or make our version of sugarplums by stuffing dates with almonds and then rolling the sticky things in sugar. I never asked for a special birthday cake. I preferred to put candles in the pumpkin pie.

In this recipe, we are basically going to make a ginger ice cream base, and then add it to pumpkin puree. Aside from a few cinnamon sticks, I am leaving out all of those other spices you are used to seeing in pumpkin pie so that the unique punch of the fresh ginger can really come through. I love using fresh pumpkin puree (see Note) for this pie, but the ready-to-use canned pumpkin works really well also.

Makes one 10-inch pie

1 prebaked 10-inch pie shell made with All-Butter Pie Dough
(page 140)
One 6 × 1-inch piece fresh ginger, unpeeled, sliced thinly, and
coarsely chopped
2 cinnamon sticks, crushed
1 cup heavy cream
¼ cup whole milk
2 large eggs
2 large egg yolks
⅔ cup sugar
½ teaspoon kosher salt
2 cups fresh or canned pumpkin puree (see **Note,** page 197)

BEFORE YOU START

Position a rack in the bottom third of your oven. Preheat the oven to 350°F.

1. In a small saucepan over medium heat, combine the ginger, crushed cinnamon sticks, heavy cream, and milk to scalding. Remove from the heat, cover, and let steep for 10 minutes. Return the saucepan to medium heat and bring back to scalding.

2. Meanwhile, in a medium bowl, whisk together the eggs, egg yolks, sugar, and salt until pale yellow. Whisk in the hot ginger cream, little by little, until combined. Strain the mixture into a clean pitcher and set aside.

3. In a separate bowl, briefly whisk the pumpkin puree until smooth. Slowly whisk in the ginger custard until incorporated.

4. Pour the pumpkin custard into the prebaked pie shell. Bake for 60 to 70 minutes, or until set—the center is no longer jiggly. Remove to a wire rack to cool.

The pie keeps tightly wrapped in plastic wrap at room temperature overnight. For longer storage, it keeps tightly wrapped in plastic warp in the refrigerator for up to 3 days (the crust will suffer slightly from the chilling).

Note: To make fresh pumpkin puree, preheat the oven to 400°F. Line a baking sheet with aluminum foil. Halve and seed a medium sugar pumpkin (5 to 6 pounds). Roast the halves cut side down on the baking sheet for 1 hour and 30 minutes, or until tender. Remove to a wire rack to cool. When cool, scrape the pulp away from the skin and puree in a food processor. Makes about 2 cups.

This is not difficult to make, but there are some steps and it does take time. The effort is well worth it, as this is one of the most silky and delicious things you will ever eat. It is very elegant.   **Makes one 8-inch cheesecake (serves 12, very rich!)**

FOR THE CRUST
½ cup all-purpose flour
2 tablespoons best-quality unsweetened Dutch-process cocoa
  powder
½ teaspoon kosher salt
½ cup sugar
¼ cup hazelnuts, chopped medium fine
3 tablespoons unsalted butter, melted
¼ cup best-quality semisweet (58%) chocolate chips

FOR THE CHEESCAKE
8 ounces best-quality bittersweet (64–68%) chocolate, coarsely
  chopped
¾ cup heavy cream
1 tablespoon plus 1 teaspoon unsweetened Dutch-process
  cocoa powder
2 tablespoons instant espresso powder
¼ teaspoon kosher salt
1 pound (two 8-ounce packages) cream cheese, at room temperature
¾ cup sugar
2 large eggs
¼ cup dark rum

FOR THE BLACKBERRY GLAZE
¼ cup blackberry or black currant preserves
1 tablespoon water

Position a rack in the center of your oven. Preheat the oven to 325°F. Turn an 8-inch springform pan upside down and cover the bottom and sides with aluminum foil. The foil should come up at least halfway on all sides, so that the water from the water bath will not leak through. Line the inside bottom of the springform pan with parchment paper cut to fit exactly. Using a nonstick vegetable cooking spray, spray the inside papered bottom and sides of the pan.

TO MAKE THE CRUST

1. In a medium bowl, combine the flour, cocoa powder, salt, sugar, and hazelnuts. Stir in the melted butter.

2. Press the mixture onto the bottom and 1 inch up the sides of the springform pan. (I use a cup with a flat base to help me press the crumbs evenly up the sides.) Bake for 15 minutes. Remove from the oven and immediately scatter the chocolate chips over the crust. Set aside until the chocolate melts, about 4 minutes. Using a small offset spatula or teaspoon, spread the chocolate evenly over the crust. Set aside to cool.

TO MAKE THE CHEESECAKE

1. Reduce the oven to 300°F.

2. In the top of a double boiler set over simmering, not boiling water, melt the chocolate, stirring occasionally. Keep warm.

3. In a small heavy-bottomed saucepan over low heat, whisk together the heavy cream, cocoa powder, espresso powder, and salt until the mixture comes to a boil. Remove from the heat and set aside to cool slightly.

4. In the bowl of an electric mixer fitted with the paddle attachment, cream together the cream cheese and sugar on medium speed until smooth, 1 to 1½ minutes. Scrape down the sides of the bowl and the paddle—*no lumps!* Pour in the melted chocolate and mix until smooth, scraping the bottom of the bowl to make sure the chocolate is incorporated. Add the cream mixture and mix well. Scrape down the sides of the bowl and the paddle again.

5. Beat in the eggs, one at a time, until just combined. Add the rum and beat until combined.

6. Pour the batter into the prepared crust and spin to level the batter. Cover the top of the springform pan with aluminum foil.

7. Place the springform pan inside a roasting pan large enough to hold it. Fill the roasting pan with hot water until it reaches halfway up the sides of the springform pan. Bake for 1 hour. Turn down the oven to 250°F and bake for an additional 45 minutes, or until the center is just set. Turn off the oven, remove the foil from the top of the cheesecake, and let the cheesecake stand in the oven for 1 more hour. (Don't open the oven door!)

8. Remove the pan from the water and place on a wire rack to cool to room temperature. Refrigerate uncovered for 3 hours to overnight before unmolding. To unmold, slide a knife along the edges of the cheesecake and release the springform pan.

9. *For the glaze:* In a small heavy-bottomed saucepan, heat the jam with water, stirring using a whisk until bubbling.

10. Strain the glaze over the chilled cheesecake and spread gently with an offset spatula. Before serving, refrigerate for approximately 10 minutes until the jam is set.

To serve, cut the cheesecake in slices using a sharp chef's knife that you've dipped in hot water, then dried with a clean towel. Garnish with fresh blackberries, if desired.

The unglazed cheesecake can be frozen in the springform pan up to 3 weeks and finished with the glazing before serving. Defrost overnight in the refrigerator. Do not unwrap before defrosting.

SPEAKEASY

I snuck a lot of booze into this cake! It is baked into the batter so it doesn't have that "liquor-soaked" taste. It is very festive, in a grown up kind of way.

Makes one 8-inch cake

FOR THE CAKE
6 ounces best-quality semisweet (58%) chocolate
10 tablespoons unsalted butter
⅔ cup brandy
4 large eggs
1⅓ cups sugar
1 cup plus 1 tablespoon all-purpose flour
1 teaspoon ground cinnamon
¼ teaspoon salt

FOR THE CHOCOLATE GLAZE
6 ounces best-quality semisweet (58%) chocolate
½ cup heavy cream
1 tablespoon light corn syrup

BEFORE YOU START

Position a rack in the center of your oven. Preheat the oven to 350°F. Lightly butter an 8 × 2-inch round cake pan. Line the bottom with an 8-inch round of parchment paper.

TO MAKE THE CAKE

1. In a medium bowl set over a pot of simmering, not boiling, water, melt the chocolate with the butter and whisk until smooth. Whisk in the brandy until smooth. Set aside to cool.

2. Separate the eggs. Place the yolks in a large mixing bowl, and the whites in an electric mixer bowl.

3. Add half of the sugar to the bowl with the yolks and whisk until thick. Add the chocolate mixture to the yolks and whisk to combine. Sift the flour, cinnamon, and salt over the chocolate batter and stir to combine.

4. In the bowl of the electric mixer fitted with the whip attachment, make a meringue by whipping the egg whites until foamy. In a slow steady stream, add the remaining sugar. Whip until the whites hold stiff but not dry peaks.

5. Briskly stir one-third of the meringue into the chocolate mixture to lighten the batter. Gently fold the remaining two-thirds of the meringue into the batter until no streaks remain.

6. Pour the batter into the prepared springform pan. Spin the pan to level the batter. Bake for 80 to 90 minutes, or until a wooden skewer inserted into the center comes out clean. (Do not do the skewer test until the cake has been baking for at least 70 minutes or you will deflate the batter!) Remove to a wire rack to cool before glazing.

TO MAKE THE GLAZE

1. When the cake is cool enough to glaze, coarsely chop the chocolate and place it in a medium bowl.

2. In a small saucepan over medium heat, heat the heavy cream until scalding, or until the cream is steaming and tiny bubbles have formed along the edges. Do not boil.

3. Pour the hot cream over the chocolate. Let stand for 5 minutes, then whisk until smooth. Stir in the corn syrup.

TO COMPLETE THE CAKE

1. Place the cake upside down on a rack set over the prepared cookie sheet.

2. Pour the glaze over the cake, letting the glaze spread itself. You may have to push it over the sides a bit, and use a small metal spatula or butter knife to smooth the sides. Try not to touch the top though, so it will be glossy and unmarred. Let the glaze set at room temperature for at least 30 minutes. Once the glaze is set, transfer the cake to a serving plate.

The cake keeps in a cake saver at room temperature for 2 days. For longer storage, refrigerate for up to 1 week.

PRO TIP: Whenever I have a batter that uses a meringue or whipped egg whites for leavening, I am not all that gentle with the first addition. The base, in this case the chocolate-yolk mixture, tends to be heavy, and the first addition of the meringue acts as a liaison, lightening the batter enough so that the rest of the meringue is accepted into the batter more easily, and can therefore retain maximum volume. So just get that first addition in however you can, then be gentle and fold the remaining meringue in properly.

Sacher Torte (My Way)

During the holidays, I chill the speakeasy (before glazing) after I bake it. Then I split it in half horizontally and spread about a ½ cup apricot preserves on top of the bottom layer. I then replace the top layer and proceed with the glazing. Try it. It's very yummy and it seems fancy. Garnish the top with whole dried apricots, if you like.

FALLEN CHOCOLATE SOUFFLÉ CAKE

This is a soufflé batter that is baked for a while, until it becomes a cake, and it's one of the most popular cakes at Sweet Melissa Pâtisserie. It is very rustic, but it looks beautiful when the "fallen" center is filled with fresh berries. **Makes one 10-inch cake**

10½ ounces best-quality semisweet (58%) chocolate
7 tablespoons unsalted butter
8 large eggs, separated
½ cup sugar divided into 2 equal parts
1 teaspoon freshly grated orange zest
1 tablespoon Grand Marnier
Confectioners' sugar, for sprinkling

BEFORE YOU START

Position a rack in the center of your oven. Preheat the oven to 350°F. Grease a 10-inch springform pan with nonstick vegetable cooking spray or butter. Line the bottom with a parchment paper round.

1. In the top of a double boiler set over simmering, not boiling, water, melt the chocolate with the butter, stirring until smooth.

2. In the bowl of an electric mixer fitted with the whip attachment, whip the egg yolks with half of the sugar until doubled in volume. Add the melted chocolate and mix until combined. Add the zest and Grand Marnier and mix until combined. Transfer the chocolate batter to a large bowl. (Wash the mixer bowl and whip attachment very well, and dry thoroughly.)

3. In the clean bowl of the electric mixer, fitted with the clean whip attachment, make a meringue by whipping the egg whites until foamy. In a slow steady stream, add the remaining sugar. Whip until the whites hold stiff but not dry peaks.

4. Briskly fold one-third of the meringue into the chocolate mixture to lighten the batter. Gently fold the remaining two-thirds of the meringue into the batter until it is just incorporated.

5. Pour the batter into the prepared springform pan. Spin the pan to level the batter. Bake for 65 minutes, or until a wooden skewer inserted into the center comes out clean. The cake will fall as it cools.

6. When the cake is cool, release the springform ring and remove it. To release the bottom, invert the cake onto a flat plate and remove the bottom and the parchment round. Turn right side up onto a serving plate and dust with confectioners' sugar.

Serve with vanilla ice cream or warm hot fudge sauce (page 185) and garnish with fresh berries, if you'd like to make the dessert a little fancy. The cake keeps tightly wrapped in plastic wrap at room temperature for up to 3 days. For longer storage, refrigerate wrapped in plastic wrap for up to 1 week. (Leave the cake in the pan for storing; it is delicate.)

CHOCOLATE RASPBERRY TRUFFLE TORTE

I love the simplicity of this torte. It really highlights the use of exceptional ingredients. Be sure to use the highest quality bittersweet chocolate available, and raspberries that are fresh and plump. It doesn't bake for long, and the resulting luxurious texture will remind you of truffles. For extra indugence, serve with Raspberry Sauce (page 176).

Makes one 8-inch torte

8 ounces best-quality bittersweet (64–68%) chocolate
8 tablespoons (1 stick) unsalted butter
3 tablespoons rum
3 large eggs
½ dry pint fresh raspberries
1 tablespoon best-quality unsweetened Dutch-process cocoa
  powder, for sprinkling

BEFORE YOU START

Position a rack in the center of your oven. Preheat oven to 350°F. Turn an 8-inch spring-form pan upside down and cover the bottom and sides with aluminum foil. The foil should come up at least 2 inches on all sides, so the water from the water bath will not leak through. Lightly butter the inside bottom and sides of the springform pan. Line the bottom with an 8-inch round of parchment paper.

1. In the top of a double boiler set over simmering, not boiling, water, gently melt the chocolate with the butter, stirring until smooth. Heat until it is just melted; don't let it get too hot. When the chocolate is fully melted, stir in the rum.

2. In an electric mixer bowl set over a pot of simmering, not boiling, water, heat the eggs while stirring until *just* warm to the touch. Remove from the heat.

3. In the electric mixer fitted with the whip attachment beat the eggs until tripled in volume, or when they reach soft peaks.

4. Fold half of the eggs into the chocolate mixture until almost incorporated. Fold in the remaining eggs until just blended but with no streaks remaining.

5. Pour half of the batter into the prepared springform pan. Scatter the fresh raspberries evenly over the batter, and then pour the remaining batter over the berries. Smooth with a spatula.

6. Place the springform pan in a roasting pan large enough to hold it. Fill the roasting pan with hot water until it reaches halfway up the sides of the springform pan. Bake uncovered for 5 minutes. Cover the pan with aluminum foil or an upside-down cookie sheet and bake for 20 minutes more. Remove to a wire rack, uncover the pan, and cool in the water bath for 1 hour.

7. Remove the pan from the water bath. Cover with plastic wrap and refrigerate until very firm, about 3½ hours.

8. Using a sharp knife, carefully loosen the cake from the edges of the pan. Release the springform ring to unmold the cake. To release the bottom, invert the cake onto a flat plate lined with parchment paper or aluminum foil and remove the bottom and the parchment round. Turn the cake right side up onto a serving plate and dust with sifted cocoa powder. Keep refrigerated before serving.

Slice with a hot knife and serve. The torte keeps tightly wrapped in plastic wrap in the refrigerator for up to 4 days.

*This is the perfect cake for a hot summer birthday party. But only if you have a freezer!
It needs to stay frozen right up until the time you are ready to slice it.*

Makes one 9-inch cake

3 tablespoons melted unsalted butter

1¼ cups vanilla wafer crumbs (about 40 cookies)

6 large eggs, separated

One 14-ounce can sweetened condensed milk

¼ teaspoon kosher salt

½ cup fresh lemon juice (about 3 lemons)

Zest of 1 lemon

½ teaspoon cream of tartar

½ cup sugar

1 recipe Fresh Strawberry Sauce (page 210)

BEFORE YOU START

Position a rack in the center of your oven. Preheat the oven to 350°F. Lightly butter the sides and base of a 9-inch springform pan. Line the bottom with a 9-inch round of parchment paper

1. In a small bowl, pour the melted butter over the wafer crumbs and stir to combine.

2. Gently press the crumb mixture into the bottom of the prepared springform pan. Do not pack in *too* tight. Bake for 12 minutes. Remove to a wire rack to cool.

3. Increase the oven temperature to 425°F.

4. In a large bowl, whisk together the egg yolks, condensed milk, salt, lemon juice, and zest.

5. Set the mixture over a pot of simmering, not boiling, water. Cook, whisking continuously until thick and fluffy, 10 to 15 minutes. Remove from the heat and set aside.

6. In the bowl of an electric mixer fitted with the whip attachment, beat the egg whites and cream of tartar until foamy. In a slow steady stream, add the sugar, beating until the whites are stiff and glossy peaks of meringue.

7. Gently fold half of the meringue into the lemon mixture. Pour the mixture into the baked crust. Spread the remaining meringue evenly over the lemon mixture, not letting it touch the sides of the pan. Bake for 8 to 10 minutes, or until the meringue is nicely browned. Remove to a wire rack to cool to room temperature. Do not remove or loosen the springform pan. When cool, freeze uncovered in its pan for at least 4 hours or overnight.

8. Slide a hot knife around the edges of the cake to loosen. Remove the springform ring to unmold the cake. To release the bottom, invert the cake onto a flat plate and remove the bottom and the parchment round. Turn right side up onto a serving plate. Serve frozen with the fresh strawberry sauce. The cake keeps frozen tightly wrapped in plastic wrap and then aluminum foil for up to 2 weeks.

FRESH STRAWBERRY SAUCE

Makes about 1 cup sauce

1 dry pint fresh strawberries, rinsed and hulled
2 tablespoons sugar
1 teaspoon fresh lemon juice
2 tablespoons cold water

1. In a food processor or blender, puree the berries, sugar, lemon juice, and water until smooth.

2. Strain the berry mixture into a clean bowl and discard the seeds. Stir in additional sugar, if needed.

3. Cover and refrigerate until ready to serve.

CHAPTER SIX

FAVORITE GIFTS

Truffles, Brittles, and Candies

Peanut Butter Truffles

Earl Grey Tea Truffles

Rum Truffles

Hazelnut Truffles

Butterscotch Pralines

Butter Toffee Crunch

Pistachio Opera Fudge

Sweet Melissa's Peanut Brittle

Peanut Praline

Roasted Cashew Brittle

Honey Cream Caramels

Chocolate Cream Caramels

Chocolate Peppermint Meringues

THERE IS NOTHING more special than a handmade gift, especially one you can eat! In this time of overabundance and instant gratification, taking the time out to make something delicious for someone special means a lot more than searching for something (anything!) in the department store just so you can cross that name off your list.

Cookies are always great to bake as gifts, and you'll find plenty in Chapter 2. But the recipes in this chapter are even more special for gift giving because they are things that people rarely make on their own. Honey Cream Caramels, Butterscotch Pralines, Peanut Butter Truffles, Chocolate Peppermint Meringues—you can't buy these presents. They are impressive to give, they are easy to make and the ingredients don't cost much at all. Pack them in a pretty

box lined with wax paper, and tie the box with a ribbon. Just be sure to attach a note, giving the gift recipient permission not to share: "These are a gift that I made for you; feel free to keep them all to yourself." But keep in mind that *your* present list may grow a little longer next year.

PEANUT BUTTER TRUFFLES

I'll bet you know someone who would love to receive these truffles as a gift even more than they would like a cashmere sweater! I love rolling these sweet truffles in the chopped salted peanuts. The sweet and salty combination tastes terrific.

Makes about 5 dozen truffles

12 ounces best-quality bittersweet (64–68%)chocolate
1¾ cups heavy cream
¼ cup peanut butter, smooth or chunky
5 tablespoons unsalted butter, softened
2 cups roasted salted peanuts, finely chopped, for rolling

1. Chop the chocolate into small pieces and put in a large bowl.

2. In a small saucepan over medium heat, heat the heavy cream and peanut butter while stirring to scalding, or until the cream is steaming and tiny bubbles have formed along the edges. Do not boil. Whisk until smooth.

3. Pour the hot peanut butter cream over the chocolate to cover completely. Set aside for 5 minutes, and then whisk until smooth.

4. Whisk in the butter to the still-warm chocolate mixture until smooth.

5. Refrigerate uncovered until the truffle base is firm enough to scoop, at least 2 hours. Using a small #100 cookie scoop or a teaspoon, scoop out the truffle base, and form into balls by rolling them around quickly in your hands.

6. Place the chopped peanuts in a shallow soup bowl. Roll each truffle in the peanuts to cover.

The truffles are best eaten at room temperature. They keep refrigerated in an airtight container for up to 2 weeks. Let come to room temperature before serving.

EARL GREY TEA TRUFFLES

These are very sophisticated truffles; they are lovely to eat. They are perfect for little ones to make and give to their tea-loving grandmas. They are also easy to make.

Makes about 5 dozen truffles

> 1 pound best-quality bittersweet (64–68%) chocolate
> 2 cups heavy cream
> 3 tablespoons loose Earl Grey tea leaves, or the tea leaves from 7 tea bags
> 5 tablespoons unsalted butter, softened
> ½ cup best-quality unsweetened Dutch-process cocoa powder, for rolling

1. Chop the chocolate into small pieces and put in a large bowl.

2. In a small saucepan over medium heat, heat the heavy cream and tea leaves to scalding. Turn off the heat, cover, and allow to steep for 15 minutes.

3. Return the cream to the heat and bring to scalding again. Strain the cream over the chocolate to cover completely. Set aside for 5 minutes and then whisk until smooth.

4. Whisk in the butter to the still-warm chocolate mixture until smooth.

5. Refrigerate until the truffle base is firm enough to scoop, at least 2 hours. Using a small #100 cookie scoop or a teaspoon, scoop out the truffle base, and form into balls by rolling them around quickly in your hands.

6. Place the cocoa powder in a shallow soup bowl. Roll each truffle in the cocoa powder to cover.

The truffles are best eaten at room temperature. They keep refrigerated in an airtight container for up to 1 month. Let come to room temperature before serving.

RUM TRUFFLES

These are one of the first truffles I ever made for Sweet Melissa's. I sell them by the piece as well as by the box, so it's not uncommon for customers to come in and order just one.

"I don't need a bag," they'll say, and pop it right into their mouth.

Makes about 4 dozen truffles

12 ounces best-quality bittersweet (64–68%) chocolate
20 tablespoons (2½ sticks) unsalted butter
4 large egg yolks
¼ cup rum
½ cup best-quality unsweetened Dutch-process cocoa powder,
  for rolling

1. Chop the chocolate into small pieces and put in a large bowl with the butter. Set the bowl over a pot of simmering, not boiling, water and stir to melt.

2. When melted and smooth, remove from the heat. Add the egg yolks and rum, and whisk until shiny and smooth.

3. Refrigerate until the truffle base is firm enough to scoop, at least 2 hours. Using a small #100 cookie scoop or a teaspoon, scoop out the truffle base, and form into balls by rolling quickly in your hands.

4. Place the cocoa powder in a shallow soup bowl. Roll each truffle in the cocoa powder to cover.

The truffles are best eaten at room temperature. They keep refrigerated in an airtight container for up to 1 month. Let come to room temperature before serving.

HAZELNUT TRUFFLES

Chocolate and hazelnuts is a classic combination. It is a little more sophisticated than the peanut butter and chocolate combination, but just as good. Give these to the mother-in-law who has everything. I assure you, she hasn't had these.

Makes about 4½ dozen truffles

3½ cups blanched hazelnuts or filberts
14 ounces best-quality semisweet (58%) chocolate
1 cup heavy cream
2 tablespoons hazelnut liqueur, such as
  Frangelico

BEFORE YOU START

Position a rack in the center of your oven. Preheat the oven to 350°F.

1. Spread the hazelnuts out on a cookie sheet and toast for about 10 minutes. Set aside to cool.

2. Chop the chocolate into small pieces and put in a large bowl.

3. In a small saucepan over medium heat, heat the heavy cream to scalding, or until the cream is steaming and tiny bubbles have formed along the edges. Do not boil. Immediately pour over the chocolate to cover. Set aside for 5 minutes.

4. Place 1½ cups of the hazelnuts in a resealable plastic bag, seal tightly, and tap the nuts with a rolling pin until they are finely crushed. (Alternatively, when the hazelnuts are very cool, pulse chop them in the bowl of a food processor.)

5. Whisk the chocolate cream mixture until smooth. Stir in the liqueur and the crushed hazelnuts until blended.

6. Refrigerate until the truffle base is firm enough to scoop, at least 2 hours.

7. Place the remaining 2 cups of hazelnuts in another resealable plastic bag, seal tightly, and tap the nuts with the rolling pin until they are finely crushed. (Alternatively, as before, when the hazelnuts are very cool, pulse chop them in the bowl of a food processor.) Transfer the crushed nuts to a shallow soup bowl.

8. Roll each truffle in the chopped hazelnuts to cover.

The truffles are best eaten at room temperature. They keep refrigerated in an airtight container for up to 2 weeks.

BUTTERSCOTCH PRALINES

Not long ago, my boyfriend and I were driving back to New York from Florida, a trip we make every winter. This time, we broke up the monotony by stopping in Savannah, Georgia—and I'm so glad we did, what a beautiful city! And, oh, the pralines. . . . I bought a bunch of freshly made pralines to bring back to my pastry cooks, and they were gone before the end of the day. I figured since my pastry cooks gobbled them up so fast, my customers might like them, too. But I had to add a twist, just to make them my own.

These butterscotch pralines make a really delicious gift. If you give them as a present, be sure to tell the recipient that they are even better if you crumble them on top of vanilla ice cream. (Or you can just keep them for yourself and put them on top of my Brown Sugar Vanilla Ice Cream, page 184.)

Makes 2 dozen pralines

2 cups granulated sugar
1 cup firmly packed light brown sugar
¾ cup water
¼ cup light corn syrup
1 teaspoon white vinegar
1 teaspoon pure vanilla extract
½ teaspoon kosher salt
1 cup butterscotch morsels
1¼ cups pecan pieces

BEFORE YOU START

Line two cookie sheets with parchment paper or aluminum foil.

1. In a medium heavy-bottomed saucepan, stir together the granulated sugar, brown sugar, water, corn syrup, vinegar, vanilla, and salt. Bring to a boil, without further stirring, until the mixture reaches 238°F on a candy thermometer. Remove from the heat.

2. Immediately transfer the hot mixture to the bowl of an electric mixer fitted with the paddle attachment. Beat in the butterscotch morsels on medium speed until the morsels are melted and the mixture is smooth and creamy. Stir in the pecans.

3. Immediately drop by tablespoonfuls (or a 1-ounce (#40) cookie scoop works even better!) onto parchment paper or aluminum foil. (If the mixture in the bowl gets too firm, you can put it back in the saucepan and melt it carefully while stirring over low heat.)

4. Let the pralines stand at room temperature to set, 5 to 10 minutes.

The pralines keep in an airtight container at room temperature, layered between sheets of wax paper, for up to 2 weeks.

BUTTER TOFFEE CRUNCH

This toffee crunch is a great gift at holiday time, and a really special birthday present as well. It is surprising how rarely people receive handmade treats for presents, and even more surprising how easy it is to make something thoughtful and delicious. This toffee crunch is guaranteed to make good friends smile.

Makes 3 pounds toffee crunch

1½ **cups sliced blanched almonds, finely chopped**
4¼ **cups firmly packed light brown sugar**
5 **tablespoons water**
20 **tablespoons (2½ sticks) unsalted butter**
1 **tablespoon pure vanilla extract**
¾ **teaspoon baking soda, sifted**
2 **cups (one 12-ounce bag) semisweet (58%)**
  chocolate chips

BEFORE YOU START

Lightly butter a jelly-roll pan or rimmed cookie sheet.

1. Coat the prepared pan with half of the chopped almonds.

2. In a large heavy-bottomed saucepan over high heat, stir together the brown sugar, water, and butter and bring to a boil. Cover for 3 minutes (this will melt any sugar crystals stuck on the sides of the pan, which will prevent crystallization). Uncover, attach a candy thermometer, and cook, without stirring, to 290°F. Watch carefully after it reaches 280°F to avoid scorching.

3. Have ready a long-handled spoon and a buttered metal offset spatula. Remove the hot sugar from the heat, add the vanilla and baking soda, and stir with the long-handled spoon (the mixture will bubble up when you add the baking soda).

4. Immediately pour the hot toffee onto the prepared pan. Spread as evenly as possible with the buttered metal spatula. Quickly scatter the chocolate chips over the hot toffee. Wait for 5 minutes and then spread the melted chocolate evenly with a clean, ungreased metal spatula.

5. Sprinkle the remaining almonds over the chocolate. Cool completely before breaking the toffee into pieces.

The toffee crunch keeps in an airtight container at room temperature in a cool dry place for up to 1 week, or in the refrigerator for up to 3 weeks.

PISTACHIO OPERA FUDGE

I love this old-fashioned fudge. You can use any kind of nut, but I love the green of the pistachios. This takes a lot of stirring by hand because a mixer just doesn't have the same result. You can skip the gym the day you make opera fudge.

Makes 16 squares fudge

4 cups sugar
1⅓ cups whole milk
¼ cup light corn syrup
½ teaspoon kosher salt
1 tablespoon pure vanilla extract
4 tablespoons (½ stick) unsalted butter
1 cup shelled unsalted pistachios, coarsely chopped

BEFORE YOU START

Butter an 8 × 8 × 2-inch square cake pan.

1. In a large (6-quart) nonreactive saucepan over medium heat, combine the sugar, milk, corn syrup, and salt. Stir until the mixture comes to a simmer. Cover and let simmer for 3 minutes.

2. Uncover and bring to a boil. Do not stir. When it reaches 238°F on a candy thermometer (soft-ball stage), remove from the heat. Let the pan cool on a wire rack—again, do not stir—until it reaches 110°F on a candy thermometer.

3. Once it has reached 110°F, with a wooden spoon, stir in the vanilla and butter until creamy, about 15 minutes. (You may want to call in some help from the kids for this part!) The fudge will start out shiny and slightly blond in color. As you stir it and in-corporate air, the fudge will lose its gloss and become lighter and thicker.

4. Stir in the pistachios.

5. Transfer the fudge to the prepared pan, and spread evenly by pressing with clean hands. Lay a sheet of plastic wrap flush against the surface of the fudge and set aside for 2 hours, or until thoroughly cooled and set.

6. When cooled, unmold the fudge and cut it into 2-inch squares.

PRO TIP: To give fudge as a present, wrap each square in wax paper and place it in an airtight tin. It will keep at room temperature for up to 2 weeks. Do not refrigerate or freeze the fudge.

SWEET MELISSA'S PEANUT BRITTLE

Peanut brittle is one of the most versatile ingredients in Sweet Melissa's kitchen. I know, that may be surprising. But we love to eat it au natural, or chopped into fine chunks and pressed onto the sides of a peanut butter–frosted layer cake (see page 100), or ground into a praline and sprinkled on hot fudge sundaes (see pages 185 and 220), or on top of butterscotch pudding (see page 180) . . . you get the idea! (This recipe involves making caramel, so be careful—no kids in the room. Hot sugar is a very bad burn.)

Makes about 2 pounds peanut brittle

1½ teaspoons baking soda, sifted
¼ teaspoon kosher salt
1 cup light corn syrup
2 cups sugar
½ pound shelled roasted peanuts
1 teaspoon pure vanilla extract
8 tablespoons (1 stick) unsalted butter, at room temperature, cut
   into ½-inch pieces

BEFORE YOU START

Lightly butter a jelly-roll pan or rimmed cookie sheet.

1. In a small bowl, whisk together the baking soda and salt.

2. In a large saucepan over medium-high heat, stir together the corn syrup and sugar and bring to a boil. When it is boiling, cover for 3 minutes (this will melt any sugar crystals stuck on the sides of the pan, which will prevent crystallization).

3. Remove the cover and cook until it reaches 348°F on a candy thermometer.

4. Remove from the heat and stir in the peanuts. Stir in the baking soda mixture. (Be careful! The mixture will bubble up and is really hot.) When the mixture starts to settle, stir in the vanilla and butter briskly, until it disappears.

5. Pour the mixture into the prepared jelly-roll pan. Spread evenly with a buttered spatula. Let cool to room temperature.

6. When completely cool, crack the brittle into irregular chunks by banging the pan flat on the counter!

Do not refrigerate or freeze. The peanut brittle keeps in an airtight container at room temperature for up to 3 weeks.

Peanut Praline

If you are using the brittle for sundaes, reserve some chunks for garnish. Then grind the remaining brittle into a coarse peanut praline in the food processor. You do not need to grind it very fine; some small chunks are good! Alternate layers of vanilla ice cream, hot fudge sauce (see page 185), and peanut praline. Garnish with chunks of peanut brittle. Enjoy!

Roasted Cashew Brittle

Just use cashews instead of peanuts and follow the recipe as directed. Delicious!

HONEY CREAM CARAMELS

I used to love to eat individually wrapped caramels when I was a kid. I thought they were magic. The great thing about them is that they teach you patience. You have to carefully unwrap the plastic, by far the most difficult part, before you can gobble them up. These caramels are made with pure honey and cream, and they are delicious. I like to wrap mine in wax paper; they are a little easier to open!

**Makes 2½ pounds caramel,
enough for sixteen 2-inch squares,
or sixty-four 1-inch squares**

1 cup light corn syrup
⅓ cup clover honey
2⅓ cups sugar
¼ teaspoon kosher salt
2 cups heavy cream
1 tablespoon unsalted butter
1 teaspoon pure vanilla extract

BEFORE YOU START

Lightly butter an 8 × 8 × 2-inch square pan.

1. In a large nonreactive saucepan over medium heat, combine the corn syrup, honey, sugar, salt, heavy cream, and butter. Cook, stirring continuously, until the mixture reaches 250°F on a candy thermometer (firm-ball stage). Remove from the heat.

2. Stir in the vanilla.

3. Pour the caramel into the prepared pan. Set aside, uncovered, in a cool place to firm up.

4. When firm, loosen the edges of the pan with a buttered knife. Turn out onto a clean work surface and, using a lightly buttered chef's knife, cut into squares.

Wrap each square in wax paper. The caramels keep in an airtight container in a cool dry place for 2 weeks.

Chocolate Cream Caramels

Cook the caramel to 248°F on a candy thermometer, then add the vanilla and 4 ounces best-quality unsweetened chocolate, finely chopped, to the hot caramel mixture. Stir until smooth. Proceed as directed.

CHOCOLATE PEPPERMINT MERINGUES

Usually meringues are made when our kitchen has a lot of egg whites left over, after the yolks have been used for ice cream and custard bases. Nothing gets wasted in a professional kitchen! These meringues are so delicious that you won't want to wait for "extra whites" in order to make them. Now, what to do with the yolks? (Hint: The Butterscotch Pudding [page 180] rocks.) Note: You will need an 18-inch pastry bag for this recipe and a ¾-inch round tip. **Makes 1½ dozen cookies**

FOR THE MERINGUES
1½ ounces best-quality bittersweet (64–68%) chocolate
2 tablespoons confectioners' sugar
5 large egg whites
1 cup sugar
Pinch cream of tartar
½ teaspoon pure vanilla extract

FOR THE PEPPERMINT GANACHE FILLING
4 ounces best-quality semisweet (58%) chocolate
2 tablespoons heavy cream
3 drops pure peppermint oil (or to your taste)

BEFORE YOU START

Position a rack in the top and bottom thirds of your oven. Preheat the oven to 200°F. Line two cookie sheets with parchment paper or aluminum foil. Fit an 18-inch pastry bag with a ¾-inch round tip (I use an Ateco #829).

TO MAKE THE MERINGUES

1. Using a serrated bread knife, finely cut the chocolate by hand (you should get about ⅓ cup). In the bowl of a food processor fitted with the metal blade, combine the chocolate and confectioners' sugar. Pulse into a fine powder. (Be careful not to process it too long or the mixture will melt!)

2. In the bowl of an electric mixer, combine the egg whites, sugar, and cream of tartar. Set the bowl over a pot of simmering, not boiling, water and whisk constantly until

the sugar is dissolved and the whites are warm to the touch (feel for sugar grains with your fingers).

3. Transfer the bowl to the electric mixer fitted with the whip attachment. Starting on low, and gradually increasing the speed to high, whip the mixture until the meringue is cool and holds stiff glossy peaks, then add the vanilla. Remove from the mixer and sprinkle the chocolate powder over the meringue; gently fold together.

4. Fill the pastry bag with the meringue. Pipe the meringue into 2-inch-wide mounds, spaced about 1½ inches apart, on the prepared cookie sheets. Bake for 1 hour and 15 minutes. Rotate the pans, then reduce the oven to 175°F. Leave the meringues in the oven for another hour, or until completely dry to the touch, but not browned. (You will know the meringues are ready when you try to lift one and it easily pulls away from the parchment paper.) Remove to a wire rack to cool completely.

TO MAKE THE GANACHE

In a medium bowl, combine the chopped chocolate and heavy cream. Set the bowl over a pot of simmering, not boiling, water, to melt the chocolate. When melted, whisk until smooth. Stir in the peppermint oil. Set aside to cool to room temperature.

TO COMPLETE THE MERINGUES

1. Remove the paper from the meringues by holding each meringue with one hand as you reach under and peel the paper from the bottom, rather than trying to lift the meringue off of the paper.

2. Turn half of the meringues upside down onto a freshly lined cookie sheet. Spread the bottoms with about ¾ teaspoon ganache. (Alternatively, use a pastry tube fitted with an Ateco #801 ¼-inch round pastry tip and pipe about ¾ teaspoon ganache onto each bottom.) Top with the remaining half of the meringues, right side up, and sandwich together the two meringues.

3. Refrigerate for 15 minutes to set before serving.

Do not refrigerate or freeze. The cookies keep in an airtight container at room temperature for up to 2 weeks.

INDEX